and Sell Overseas

Better Business Guides

Getting to Yes Roger Fisher and William Ury

Effective Delegation Clive T. Goodworth

The Telephone Marketing Book Pauline Marks

The Basic Arts of Financial Management *Third Edition* Leon Simons

The Basic Arts of Marketing *Second Edition* Ray L. Willsmer

Janner's Complete Letterwriter Greville Janner

Janner's Complete Speechmaker *Second Edition* Greville Janner

Janner on Presentation Greville Janner

The Small Business Finance Raiser Stan Mason

Negotiate Anywhere Gavin Kennedy

How to Buy and Sell Overseas Tom Cannon and Mike Willis

Do Your Own Advertising Alastair Crompton

How to Win Profitable Business Tom Cannon

How to Manage People Ron Johnson

How to Buy and Sell Overseas

Tom Cannon and Mike Willis

Hutchinson Business
London Melbourne Auckland Johannesburg

Hutchinson Business
An imprint of Century Hutchinson Ltd
62-65 Chandos Place, London WC2N 4NW

Century Hutchinson Australia PTY Ltd
16-22 Church Street, Hawthorn, Melbourne, Victoria 3122

Century Hutchinson Group (NZ) Ltd
32-34 View Road, PO Box 40-086, Glenfield, Auckland 10

Century Hutchinson Group (SA) PTY Ltd
PO Box 337, Bergvlei 2012, South Africa

First published 1986
Reprinted 1987

© Tom Cannon and Mike Willis 1986

Set in Helvetica by Words & Pictures Ltd,
Thornton Heath, Surrey

Printed and bound in Great Britain by
The Guernsey Press Co. Ltd,
Guernsey, Channel Islands

British Library Cataloguing in Publication Data

Cannon, Tom
    How to buy and sell overseas and boost your export business.
    — (Better business guides)
    1. Export marketing — Great Britain
    2. Small business — Great Britain
    3. Great Britain — C,
    I. Title II. Willis, Mike III. Series
    658.8′48′0941   HF1009.5

ISBN 0–09–172221–7

Contents

Acknowledgements		11
Foreword		12
Introduction		13
1	**What Growth Routes are Open to My Business?**	**17**
	Introduction and aims	17
	Why do you want growth?	18
	The growth options	19
	Strategic choice	24
	Summary	25
	Action guidelines	27
2	**Purchasing and Licensing from Overseas**	**29**
	Introduction and aims	29
	Why import?	31
	How to purchase from overseas	33
	Assessing overseas suppliers	35
	Distributing goods for overseas principals	36
	Licensing and cross-licensing	36
	Summary	37
	Action guidelines	39
3	**The Export Experience Base**	**41**
	Introduction and aims	41
	Past inquiries	43
	Experience of managing intermediaries	45
	Competitors' experience	45
	Summary	45
	Action guidelines	47
4	**Your Commitment: the Key Resource**	**50**
	Introduction and aims	50
	Think positive	50
	Getting started	52

	Summary	56
	Action guidelines	58
5	**Mobilizing Export Resources**	**61**
	Introduction and aims	61
	What can I offer for export?	62
	Product/service analysis	62
	Financial resources for exports	67
	Analysing strengths and weaknesses	68
	Summary	68
	Action guidelines	72
6	**Using the Firm's Network**	**74**
	Introduction and aims	74
	Understanding the network	75
	Effectively managing the network	77
	Export organizations	79
	Summary	81
	Action guidelines	82
7	**Selecting Export Opportunities**	**86**
	Introduction and aims	86
	Personal priority	87
	Maximizing returns from existing contracts	94
	Simple elimination	95
	Summary	110
	Action guidelines	111
8	**Using the Government Support Agencies**	**113**
	Introduction and aims	113
	The British Overseas Trade Board (BOTB)	114
	What can the BOTB do for me?	118
	Other government services	123
	Summary	126
	Action guidelines	128
9	**Using the Commercial Support Services**	**129**
	Introduction and aims	129
	Bank services to exporters	129
	Trade associations	132
	The CBI	134
	Chambers of commerce and industry	135
	Industry research associations	136
	The British Standards Institution	137
	Other agencies	138

	Summary	139
	Action guidelines	140
10	**Managing Market Research**	141
	Introduction and aims	141
	Information and data sources	142
	Doing your own research	146
	Using external consultants	147
	Summary	148
	Action guidelines	149
11	**'Armchair' Exporting**	152
	Introduction and aims	152
	Subcontracting	153
	Consortia	154
	The Crown Agents	154
	Foreign buyers	155
	Export houses	156
	Export management companies	156
	'Piggy-back' exporting	157
	Summary	157
	Action guidelines	158
12	**Getting the Most out of Agents and Distributors**	159
	Introduction and aims	159
	The agent's function	160
	Recruitment of agents	161
	Management of agents	164
	Motivation of agents	165
	Control of agents	167
	Distributors	168
	Summary	169
	Action guidelines	171
13	**Financing Exports**	175
	Introduction and aims	175
	Pre-shipment finance	176
	Post-shipment finance	179
	Simplifying export finance for the smaller firm	180
	Export Credits Guarantee Department (ECGD)	181
	Summary	183
	Action guidelines	184
14	**Administration for Exports**	185

	Introduction and aims	185
	The contractual terms	187
	The trading process: associated documents	192
	Simplification of International Trade Procedures (SITPRO)	196
	Summary	197
	Action guidelines	200
15	**Communicating with Overseas Markets**	201
	Introduction and aims	201
	Letter contact	202
	Using the phone	202
	Telex contact	204
	Personal visits	204
	Summary	205
	Action guidelines	206
16	**Managing Overseas Promotion**	207
	Introduction and aims	207
	Establishing the budget	208
	Trade fairs	208
	Overseas publicity	212
	Literature	214
	Advertising	214
	Summary	215
	Action guidelines	216
17	**Planning for Exports**	217
	Introduction and aims	217
	Getting started	219
	Setting objectives	220
	Export strategy	221
	Action plans	221
	Budgets and controls	222
	Summary	222
	Action guidelines	223
	Appendices	225
	Index	232

Acknowledgements

We would like to thank the 250+ managers we have worked with over the last five years and who have helped develop our ideas. In particular we would like to acknowledge the assistance of John Higgins of Professional Manufacturing & Distribution, Alan Dean of Advanced Lubrication Services, Mark Jones of John Mason & Son, Tony Bagley of Plastic Mouldings (Cradley), Brian Bate of Rockhurst Design Services, Henri Strzelecki of Henri-Lloyd, Gary Newell of Oilab Lubrication & Mike Fox of Wicksteed Leisure.

Our thanks to Arthur Hilton of the BOTB Secretariat, David Royce of the Institute of Export, Mr Woodward of NEDO, Mr Pulleyn of Dart Containerline, Mr Colbert of Midland Bank Tradebrief and Steven Heath of SITPRO for permission to reproduce copyright material.

Special thanks are due to our patient publisher and our understanding wives – Leonie and Fran.

Foreword

There is no better time than the present to generate interest in overseas markets. The publication of this book in Industry Year 1986 focuses attention on generating business for our nation. Industry Year 1986 is about re-awakening appreciation and understanding of what industry is all about, and of course industry includes the identification and satisfaction of markets of all types.

The authors are to be commended for producing a book which is both readable and useful – in total it provides a pragmatic overview of what international marketing is all about. At the same time it can be used for reference, for guidance on particular topics and as a training aid.

The book is aimed, as it says in its introduction, to highlight opportunities which exist for the smaller and medium-sized concerns within international markets. Indeed, the larger corporations have extensive marketing departments dedicated to the tasks of researching, planning and exploiting markets in diverse countries. It is the smaller enterprise run by the owner-manager and the companies setting out for the first time into export markets who need guidance. I strongly recommend that this book becomes required reading in the Boardroom and offices of every small and medium-sized business which has not yet, or has only just, started an international effort. Marketing internationally is rewarding – and fun!

John Parsons

John Parsons, C.Eng., is an electronic engineer by profession. In June 1985 he was appointed to the British Overseas Trade Board with a specific brief for the smaller and medium-sized company.

Introduction

This book is about winning business: its aim is to highlight the opportunities which exist for smaller and medium-sized concerns within international markets and to provide practical guidelines to help capitalize on those opportunities. These opportunities vary in form from direct exports to the location of new sources of supply which can assist development within the domestic market. A word of warning: this is not another 'how to run an import/export business', with emphasis on procedures, documentation and commercial practices. There are enough of these on the market. The book encourages a greater degree of international involvement – an alertness and responsiveness to changing overseas markets, and the opportunities this creates: an awareness/alertness to the product and service levels provided by competitor firms to their customers.

But just a minute – isn't the international market-place too grandiose an arena for the smaller firm? The force of technology has made the world a smaller place – cheaper and swifter transport, more rapid and advanced communication and regular flows of information; a world which is changing, converging and becoming more competitive. It is wrong to assert that the small firm should concern itself only with its own domestic 'patch', for even here the firm is not secure from the threats and pressures of international competition. To ignore the outside world is suicidal.

To hold out in the domestic market, firms may already compete with suppliers from overseas. In this case, they can probably compete with them on their own ground. If there is no international competition, there is no guarantee it won't occur in the future. Do you know whether your customers are aware of the products and service levels obtainable from compatible overseas suppliers? Are your customers aware of gaps in pricing, marketing support, training, help with installation, or other factors essential to your industry? If not, the customer may eventually 'switch on' and change suppliers. The recession has forced firms to:

1   Improve products/services to hold their customers.
2   Search for new customers to maintain volume.

As a result, firms are forced to look towards new markets.

Increasing international awareness for profit is central to this book. Its primary aim is to help firms develop direct export business. It will also help firms:

- Locate cheaper or more attractive sources of supply of components, raw materials and equipment.
- Locate more advanced sources of technology and equipment.
- Evaluate existing manufacturing, managerial and marketing performance against overseas firms and competition and highlight gaps for action and improvement.
- Locate new products, designs, licences, services and service levels for adoption within the domestic market.
- License and cross-license technology/products/know-how overseas.

Importing and exporting are two sides of a coin: importing is not an 'unpatriotic' activity which undermines the balance of payments. More effective buying and importing practices and procedures strengthen domestic business by reducing costs, cutting lead times and possibly providing a stronger and more efficient base to build up exports. Similarly, if firms are already exporting, and spending time overseas, this can be used as a platform to search out new suppliers and new products for the UK market. These two activities are inextricably linked and can be mutually supportive.

This book assumes you want your business to develop. By working through it and completing the exercises, it will help test the validity of this assumption and whether markets and customers overseas offer a route for development. The book does require 'working through'. Just reading it will provide hints and ideas and a broad framework on how to capitalize on overseas opportunities; but it is the completion of the exercises and action guidelines that helps translate the broad ideas and concepts to specific company circumstances and provides a way ahead in the complex task of developing business. Having worked through the book, you may conclude that, much as you like the prospect of increased exports or a wider range of suppliers, the costs involved, in both time and resources, do not justify the effort, and that overseas markets are better left alone – at least for the time being. If the book helps generate this conclusion, it will not have been a hollow exercise, for many smaller enterprises are dragged backwards into the international arena without adequate preparation or consideration. The results can be disastrous.

> A manufacturer of men's outwear was approached direct to supply Libya with 'telephone number' quantities of suiting for the Libyan military. The company had never considered exporting but at first sight the potential order was a 'gift horse' which could fill under-utilized production capacity due to a decline in the UK market. In the bitter light of experience, the order almost 'broke' the company. Senior management became involved in long, complex and expensive negotiations in Tripoli. They were beaten down on price, and the order, when it did arrive, created enormous demands on working capital. Finally there were unplanned delays on shipment and payment. The company vowed never again to touch the Libyan market and viewed exports with some scepticism.

This book is primarily aimed at the needs of owner-managers, from smaller and medium-sized enterprises, and much of the material is based on the writers' experiences of working with owner-managers to help develop the export potential of their business. In common with these managers, you will need to:

- Invest time in planning profitable business development.
- Think 'strategically' about business development.
- Be willing and able to take action.
- Be willing to take on ideas and products generated outside of the business.

Apart from owner-managers, the approach of this book will be relevant to the needs of those managers who have responsibility for exports or buying, and to senior managers from the independent subsidiaries of larger groups who share many of the characteristics of the smaller enterprise. Such managers and/or owners may be involved in overseas markets via importing or exporting and may be dissatisfied with present performance and wish to take remedial action, or unsure how to improve on existing performance; or they may not be involved overseas and want to know how to make a start. This book is a practical guide whose ideas and notions are designed to be broadly applicable, although the needs of specific industries/services are highlighted in the form of short case studies.

However much you can do yourself, there is still need for professional advice and help from outsiders. The British Overseas Trade Board (BOTB) guides and directs the government's assistance to UK exporters and provides financial assistance, specific information, and advice.

1
What Growth Routes are Open to My Business?

- Building business overseas via exporting is one of many growth options.
- Growth options are bounded by risks and challenges of a greater or lesser degree.
- A strategic choice has to be made from among these options.

Introduction and aims

This book assumes you want your business to grow and that you are looking towards overseas markets to help meet expansion plans. Many of the most exciting challenges to business come from expansion and growth. Care and attention are required if a heavy price is to be avoided. Entering into export markets requires the same consideration as any other new business venture – a gathering of all the available information on the growth options open to the firm and then, on the basis of this information, a reasoned decision on the way forward. This unit is for managers who want to explore the growth options open to them and place the risks and opportunities of entering into overseas markets firmly into context. Firms wanting a one-off export order as a lifeline will find the approach of this book unappealing. You may be lucky and an unexpected order arrives – we wish you luck. But this book is for managers who have the confidence and competence to undertake a planned development of their business, and who can make growth happen. This section will help the firm:

- Explore growth options.
- Prioritize growth options.
- Quantify the risks of entry into exporting.

Why do you want growth?

So you are thinking about growth from export markets. What exactly do you want to see grow? Tick the areas within your business you wish to see grow as a result of entering into export markets.

Export sales volume	☐
Export sales revenue	☐
Export sales gross contribution	☐
Royalty revenue	☐
Gross profit	☐
Net profit	☐
Agency network	☐
Range of products/services	☐
Number of employees	☐
Export market share	☐
Your income/salary	☐
Asset value	☐
Reserves	☐
Shareholders' fund	☐
Other: _____	

Now list the four most important areas:

1. _____
2. _____
3. _____
4. _____

Now alongside the four, detail why these areas matter. What will you use a larger agency network for? Why do you want an increase in profit before tax, and what will the funds be used for? You may wish to 'fatten the goose' in order to sell out. It is well worth establishing at this early stage what we mean by growth and why we want it. Growth is really about making changes. It is a truism that no business can stand still. We can never say, 'That's enough, I am fully satisfied with the business and the way we service our customers,' for we operate in dynamic markets which are constantly changing and which require business organizations to adapt to these changes – changes in the form of improvements and developments in products and service levels, increased productivity: in short, doing things better and realizing the full potential of the business. You may look to exporting to help maintain or consolidate the business, but the process will involve change and development.

The growth options

A useful vehicle for exploring the growth options open to the business enterprise is the match of markets/customers and products/services. Markets/customers are the major external resource of the business and products/services the major internal resource. The matrix in Figure 1 reviews the various growth options by linking up these two sets of resources.

PRODUCTS/ SERVICES	MARKETS/CUSTOMERS		
	Existing domestic	New domestic	Overseas
Existing	1	3	4
New	2	5	

Figure 1

Growth option 1: market penetration The shaded box within the matrix is the current position of the firm with its existing mix of products and services supplied to existing domestic markets/customers. In broad terms, the further one moves away from this point the higher the risk and challenges. This is particularly true of the smaller firms whose business has been built up on the basis of supplying one or two local customers. In order to grow from this base requires (1) improved marketing, and (2) improved financial control – which in turn lead to increased market penetration.

Improved financial control If there are doubts about the financial controls within the business, rectify them now. Growth – particularly via export markets – demands close financial scrutiny; and, if the controls are weak and financial information non-existent or late, then growth is likely to tear the business apart. In any case, reviewing financial controls and 'tightening up' the business can help promote short-term growth. How informed are you about the financial performance of your business?

	Very well informed	*Would like to know more*	*Not at all informed*
Weekly sales v. planned sales			
Selling prices			
Cost structures			
Debtors			
Creditors			
Stocks			
Purchase prices			
New customer vetting			
Cash flow			
Fixed assets			

If you are happy with the financial information received, fine; if not, use the action guidelines to help improve financial control of the business.

Improved marketing Earlier we described growth as making changes and making things happen: it is the marketing function that provides the direction and scope of these changes. The marketing orientated firm keeps adapting and changing to remain in tune with changing customers' needs and the dynamics of the market-place. It strives to get close to customers, establish what makes them 'tick' and supply them with what they want. This striving provides the opportunity for increased market penetration, increased profitability, and therefore growth. How informed is the firm about existing markets and customers serviced, its capability to provide them with the products and services they require relative to competitors? Use the action guidelines to measure existing marketing performance and analyse gaps for improved market penetration. A word of warning: marketing is not a function which can be delegated to one person, and it cannot be simply introduced into the business by giving the sales manager the title of sales and marketing manager. Virtually every part of the firm is involved in matching its capabilities to customer requirements, and therefore marketing should permeate right through smaller business enterprises. When applied with flair and competence, marketing provides an important avenue for increased market penetration.

Growth option 2: product development The introduction of new products and services into existing markets provides a second growth option. Smaller concerns that are often close to their products/services and have built up considerable technical competence are more likely to follow this growth route. It becomes easier to make sound judgements on the technical aspects of a new idea or product; and experiments/prototypes can often be set up quickly to endorse the feasibility of a product. For many such firms, key customers are the major source of new product ideas, which are then jointly developed. Certainly new products and services are the life-blood of any business and should form a central plank of the firm's marketing activity, but their introduction is bounded by risks and challenges. One method of reducing risk is to search for a proven product/service from overseas and negotiate a licence to sell in the UK, thus short-circuiting the expensive and time-consuming process of new product development. Licensing international products and services can contribute to growth in the UK, but it demands a methodical search pattern and investment in time overseas (see Unit 2).

Growth option 3: domestic market development There are many opportunities for taking a firm's existing products and services into entirely new domestic markets and customers.

A small rubber moulder from the South-west, an independent operating company within a large UK conglomerate, manufactures vehicle accessories and markets these to overseas export markets and wholesalers. One of these accessories is a rubber strap for exhaust systems; it was found that a slightly modified product could be sold as a support strap for young trees/saplings. The local authority sector and customers within the local government housing and recreation departments became an important new market for the firm, reducing dependence on declining OEMs.

A northern-based manufacturer of safety headwear selling to the National Coal Board looked to expand its business by developing sales of the same product to military users within the orbit of the Ministry of Defence. This reduced the firm's dependence on the declining coal industry whose ordering schedules had been disrupted by industrial disputes.

Gaining access to new customers with differing needs and foreign buying procedures, who know nothing of a new firm's ability to supply, requires a special competence and professionalism. But unlike moves into new overseas markets, there may be fewer problems of:

- Communication.
- Relationship building.
- Physical distribution.
- After-sales servicing.

Growth option 4: overseas market development Competence and professionalism are of critical importance when taking existing products/services into new and unknown markets where customers are bounded by different market environments, and where relations between UK suppliers and customers are aggravated by distance and cultural differences. If you are thinking of pursuing this growth option in order to dump redundant UK stock or to extend production runs, you had better think again. For it is more than likely that overseas customers, whether from developed or less developed economies, will require product changes to suit local market conditions, and will have different expectations and be bounded by different technical standards. There is a consequent requirement to rethink servicing levels. This can lead to an interesting 'growth loop' (see Figure 2) which can support domestic growth.

	Existing domestic	New domestic	Overseas
Existing — MARKET PENETRATION		Moves to exports lead to improvements in existing products/marketing method and licensing of new products	
New — PRODUCT DEVELOPMENT			

PRODUCTS/SERVICES (rows) — MARKETS/CUSTOMERS (columns)

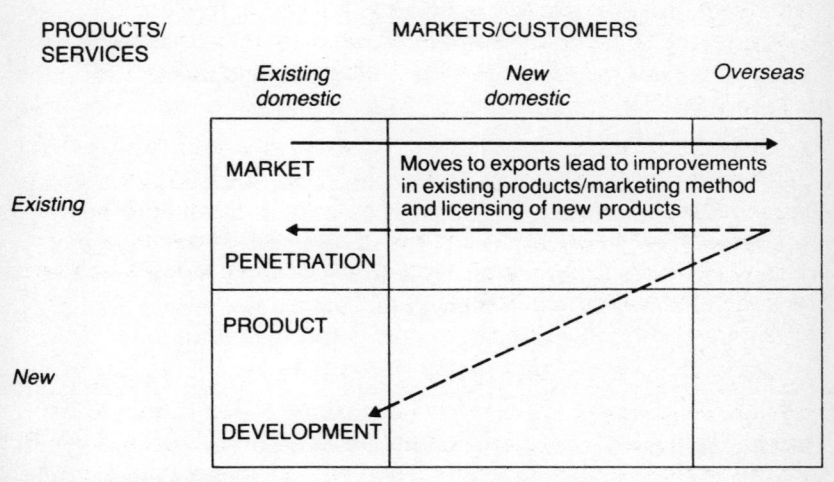

Figure 2 *Growth loop*

A Bradford-based manufacturer of office furniture, looking to the Benelux market for expansion, found that local designs and product performance were well in advance of its own range and it was unable to compete on price. However, the firm decided to apply some of the Benelux market design features to its own products and up-grade the range. This led to improved business with existing customers in the UK.

Professional Manufacturing & Distribution (PMD), a division of East Riding Engineering Co. Ltd, is a leading manufacturer of cycle, motor-cycle and car accessories. It was alerted to the opportunity of exhibiting at a Stockholm trade show which was subsidized by the British Overseas Trade Board. At that time, the PMD cycle puncture repair kits were packed in a metal box. The Swedish and other Scandinavian buyers 'laughed' at the old-fashioned style of the box and pointed out that its sharp metal edges presented a safety problem in Scandinavia. The young managing director of PMD returned to the UK without an export order but with the commitment to invest in new packaging designs and materials. The firm now has the most up-to-date computer-controlled injection moulding machine, and repair kits are now packed into plastic 'easy-close' boxes with no safety problems. This packaging innovation has led to considerable growth within the UK market.

Similarly, moves towards overseas market development alert firms to innovative marketing and promotion methods which can be applied within the UK market.

The managing director of a Midlands manufacturer of play equipment visited Sweden in search of new water-based activity products such as water slides. He found that local manufacturers were running joint promotions with fast-food chains – tickets to ride the water slides were distributed in the restaurants. The managing director decided to use this idea in the UK.

Growth option 5: diversification This requires going beyond existing markets and existing products into totally new areas. Because it takes the firm away from its major area of expertise and from the markets it knows best, this growth option is the most risky, particularly for the smaller concern.

Strategic choice

Because every growth option or route requires a particular mix of skills and strengths, and more importantly the eventual commitment of company resources, it is important that a 'strategic' choice is made. As we have seen, a firm can venture towards overseas markets with the initiative resulting in product developments which lead to growth within the domestic market; similarly success in new overseas markets improves confidence and can strengthen a firm's position within its domestic market. 'Feeling one's way' along the growth routes is fine in the short term, but to move simultaneously along all routes is unlikely to produce any real results due to the dissipation of effort and the spreading of scarce resources.

There are no hard and fast rules, but firms should carefully consider options 1, 2 and 3 before looking to develop overseas markets. Closely linked to this choice will be your own personal objectives and ambitions, the strengths and weaknesses of your own business skills and – most importantly for the owner-manager – those business activities that you enjoy getting involved in.

Summary

Developing overseas markets is one of a number of growth options. These need to be carefully considered. It poses special risks and challenges for the smaller firm as it takes them out of their usual operating environment. This is particularly true for the small subcontractor or component manufacturer whose business has been built up on supplying a small number of customers in close geographical proximity, whom they have got to know and where the relationship is efficiently managed. All growth options should be carefully considered, and a strategic choice made.

Improved marketing plays a crucial role in the planning and management of growth and development. It is marketing that enables a firm to make growth happen and keep in step with the changing market-place, whether in the domestic market or overseas. Improved financial controls, or 'tightening up', can help your performance within existing markets and are a prerequisite in the search for export opportunities.

Growth options can be graded in the light of their degree of complexity and risk.

Existing market penetration	
New product/service development	
New domestic market development	*Increasing risk*
Overseas market development	
Diversification	↓

Preliminary research in overseas markets can feed back into improved domestic performance via:

1 Licensing.
2 Cross-licensing.
3 Adoption of innovative marketing and promotional methods.
4 Improvements in products, designs, service levels, etc.

Further reading

Cannon, T., *How to Win Profitable Business* (1984), Business Books.
Eversley, J., et al., *Be Your Own Boss – Growth Kit* (1983), National Extension College.
Tolley's *Survival Kit for Small Businesses* (1981), Touche Ross & Co.

The action guidelines Not all of the check-lists and questions will apply to you. Some of the questions will suggest further questions. Use the guidelines creatively and let them assist you to take action – this is their main purpose.

Action Guidelines

1 What motivates you to strive for growth and development?
_____
_____
_____
_____

2 Using the growth options matrix, indicate where current policies are directed.

	MARKETS/CUSTOMERS		
PRODUCTS/SERVICES	*Existing domestic*	*New domestic*	*International*
Existing			
New			

3 On what basis was this option selected?
_____
_____
_____
_____

4 Can you increase existing market penetration by 'tightening up' in the following areas?

	Action by whom	*Date*
Institute a cost reduction programme		
Getting the most out of government loans, enterprise zones, tax allowances		
Review fixed assets with a view to improving utilization or more efficient financing		
What remedial action can be taken to improve cash flow?		

5   Can you increase existing market penetration by improved marketing in the following areas?

	Action by whom	Date
Frequency of sales visits		
Training sales force		
Accessibility to customers of sales/technical staff/top management		
Speed and reliability of delivery		
Warranty and after-sales service		
Advertising and promotion		
Product performance and design		
Product packaging		
Product and service value for money		

6   Compare performance in the above areas with that of competitors. Where are the biggest gaps?

_____
_____
_____

7   Appoint a 'devil's advocate' whose function will be to tell you things about your business and products you would rather not know. List the priority areas which require action and improvement.

Action	Date to be completed	By whom

8   Gather together returns, customer complaints, guarantee cards. What does this tell you about your marketing performance?

_____
_____
_____

2
Purchasing and Licensing from Overseas

- Overseas markets should be considered as important supply markets.
- International purchasing and licensing are a viable option for the smaller firm intent on developing and improving its operation.
- Importing, like exporting, requires specialist skills; outside agencies can be used to handle the task.

Introduction and aims

This book is primarily concerned with winning export business using a common-sense marketing approach, but for many firms the first involvement in overseas markets is not through exporting but importing. These two activities are not incompatible.

Marketing has been defined in many ways, but perhaps the most succinct is: *getting the right goods or services in the right quantity to the right place at the right time and at the right price*. There is a tendency to view the marketing activities of exporting firms as the only active forces directed towards passive buying organizations (see Figure 3). But in reality, the buying or importing firm can take the initiative and actively market its own purchasing/importing requirements to overseas suppliers (see Figure 4). Indeed, a well-known definition of procurement objectives is remarkably similar to the above marketing definition: *to purchase the right quality of material, at the right time in the right quantity from the right source, at the right price.*

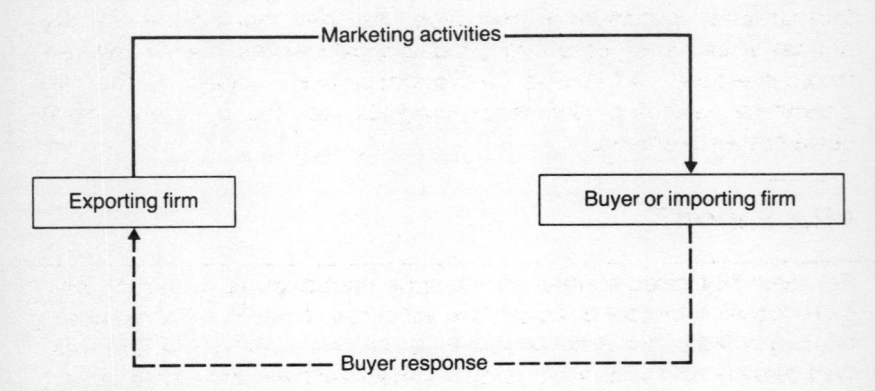

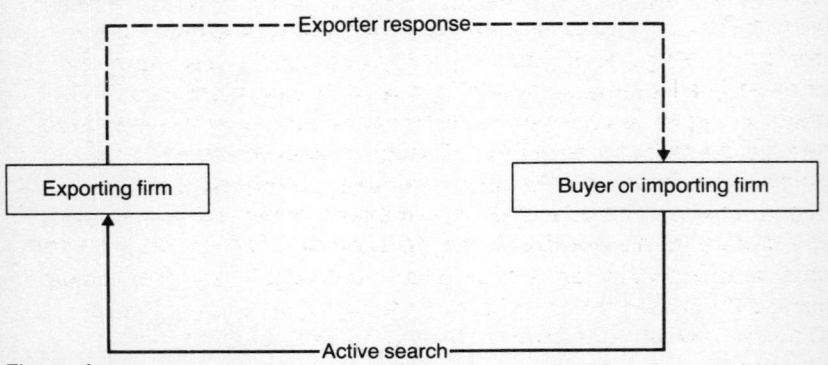

```
                 ─── Marketing activities ───
         ┌──────────────────────────────────────┐
         │                                      ▼
  ┌─────────────────┐                  ┌─────────────────────┐
  │ Exporting firm  │                  │ Buyer or importing firm │
  └─────────────────┘                  └─────────────────────┘
         ▲                                      │
         └─ ─ ─ ─ ─ ─ Buyer response ─ ─ ─ ─ ─ ─┘
```
Figure 3

```
         ┌─ ─ ─ ─ ─ Exporter response ─ ─ ─ ─ ─┐
         │                                     │
         ▼                                     │
  ┌─────────────────┐                  ┌─────────────────────┐
  │ Exporting firm  │                  │ Buyer or importing firm │
  └─────────────────┘                  └─────────────────────┘
         ▲                                     │
         └────────── Active search ────────────┘
```
Figure 4

Marketing and purchasing, exporting and importing, are inextricably linked: they form two sides of a coin. This unit is specifically concerned with aspects of purchasing/importing from abroad, but ensuing units – covering agents and distributors (Unit 12), export finance (Unit 13) and administration (Unit 14) – will be equally relevant to the importing firm, as they explain the exporter's role within the import transaction. It is too facile to condemn importing as an unpatriotic activity: the UK is an open economy depending on the purchase of raw materials and semi-manufactured items for conversion into added value items for resale or re-export. The country depends on international trade, and a rich base of importing and exporting skills has been built up. This unit explores the strategic advantages of a wider and more international purchasing approach, as well as examining the critical aspects of licensing products, processes and know-how from overseas. All these approaches assist firms further to penetrate existing domestic markets or make them more competitive overseas.

Why import?

For over fifty years a small sports-shoe manufacturer relied on its own output from three factories sited close to the boot- and shoe-making skills of the East Midlands. By the mid-1970s, the firm was well established with a range of branded, leather-uppered soccer and training shoes within the independent sports trade. It lagged well behind the West German giants – Puma and Adidas – which were locked in a fierce promotional war, but this worked to the firm's advantage, as it was increasing consumer awareness and interest in all speciality sports footwear. The problem was in the major multiples and department stores, which were gearing up to service the 'leisure revolution' through aggressive world-wide purchasing. Price was the major stumbling block: these major accounts were capable of placing massive order 'schedules' with any factory in the world, and the Koreans and Taiwanese were the most responsive in terms of price and delivery. The West German competition were quick to license manufacture of their 'basic' shoes to low-labour-cost countries such as East Germany, Yugoslavia and in the Far East, whilst retaining the manufacture of flagship, premium-priced lines within the existing West German plant and concentrating resources on research and development. This enabled them to service the specialist sports trade with higher-grade products and offer lower-cost basic shoes to the non-sports-trade accounts.

The UK firm was export orientated, with over 100 individual overseas customers and 16% of sales going to the Far East. But it insisted on relying on local output to service domestic and export markets rather than source from low-cost-labour markets. The firm was eventually driven from the market.

The West German firms in this example succeeded because they did not accept the status quo and were able to visualize the business as a linking network of supply and sales markets with them at the centre pulling the strings. The UK firm was myopic in its vision, accepting full output from domestic plant as a central plank in its operations; and it failed to incorporate creative procurement into its marketing strategy. Importing may be critical to a firm's ability to survive within the domestic market.

Considerations about importing are dependent on the nature of the firm and the markets it operates in. The following list includes a range of the reasons why firms choose to import:

- Items may be in short supply, or no longer available within the domestic market.
- There may be strategic supply reasons for importing from abroad, e.g. disruption caused by strikes.
- Imports may be cheaper due to low labour costs, economies of scale, exchange rate fluctuations, better plant, etc.
- Imports of products can complement existing lines. During the 1970s, a medium-sized manufacturer of wood-working machinery and machine tools tried to protect itself against foreign infiltration by importing equipment in areas where its own range was deficient.
- Importing to overcome gaps in new product development: Wicksteed Leisure's business was built on supplying metal playground equipment to the local authority market. Changes in preference for wooden equipment because of safety, maintenance and aesthetic factors left Wicksteed without a product to offer. To solve the short-term problem, a range of wooden products was sourced from Finland, until the company developed the Logworld range.
- To obtain access to certain export markets, there may be an element of reciprocal trading or buy-back arrangements.
- Overseas suppliers may offer improved products, better warranty and servicing, and swifter delivery.
- Firms that are exporting can combine overseas selling trips with visits to suppliers. A small men's outerwear manufacturer,

> for example, sold men's suits to the French market as well as purchasing cloth from the same country.

How to purchase from overseas

Importing offers many benefits, not least the ability to compete more effectively within the domestic market. There are of course difficulties associated with importing. A real problem is the sheer number of supplier markets, diversity of suppliers, and lack of information on the best sources of supply. Just buying at random from various suppliers in different countries will burden the firm with extra work. A more productive approach is to define purchasing requirements in terms of:

1. Raw materials.
2. Components.
3. Equipment.
4. Finished products.
5. Know-how.
6. New technology.
7. The quality, price and service levels expected.

Then a systematic approach should be developed towards identifying the sources of supply which meet company requirements. This systematic approach includes:

- **Desk research** *(see Unit 10)*
  Consult overseas trade publications
  Trade statistics
  Trade directories
  Exhibition handbooks
  Buyers' guides and yearbooks
- **Using the firm's network** *(see Unit 6)*
  Banks
  Embassies and high commissions in London (these are there to promote their countries' exports and are very helpful)
  Trade associations

> Trade development organizations, e.g. the UK-based Hong Kong Development Council
> Competitors
> Existing suppliers
> Freight forwarders
> Chambers of commerce
> Customs and Excise, Import Section, Kent House, Upper Ground, London SE1 (01-928 0533): for information on current import duties
> Department of Trade, Import Licensing Branch, Charles House, 375 Kensington High Street, London W14 8QH (01-603 4644)

From these approaches, the firm can isolate those supply markets providing (1) easy access, (2) favourable exchange rates, (3) few restrictions on importing, and most important of all (4) the ability to meet the firm's buying requirements.

It is advisable for the first-time importer to operate through an import agency. They are closer to hand, may hold local stocks and help simplify the importing process.

> **Contact point**
> British Importers' Confederation (BIC), 69 Cannon Street, London EC4N 5AB (01-248 4444).

Once the confidence has been built up, the firm can begin to deal direct with overseas sources of supply, but should take into account:

> - *Time* The amount of time required to deal direct and the opportunity cost within the business.
> - *Workload* The additional workload in handling import procedures and documentation.
> - *Skills* Are there the skills internally to cope with this workload, or is training required?
> - *Lead times* It can take many weeks to ship goods from the Far East.

Assessing overseas suppliers

Negotiations with overseas sources of supply should take into account:

1 Quality.
2 Quantity.
3 Price.
4 After-sales service.
5 Delivery.

} *That is, the ability to meet your needs/specification.* {

The basic approaches for assessing a supplier's capability are based on (1) reputation and (2) a visit and appraisal. Overseas suppliers may have built up a reputation, and it is important to verify this by taking up references. Where no reputation exists, a visit will be necessary. Third-party certification such as the UK BS 5179 may be available to assess independently supplier capability (see below: 'Trade associations', page 132; and 'The British Standards Institution', page 137). The visit should be used to assess thoroughly the capability of the supplying firm to meet your requirements or specification. This will cover the overall state of the plant and equipment, quality control systems, quality of work in progress, quality of management, etc. (see Unit 5 for a short case study covering a visit and supplier appraisal). The firm will want to obtain quotations from a selection of suppliers to compare with one another and with quotations from the UK. The cheapest quotation may not necessarily be the best match for your requirements; quality and delivery are likely to feature as more critical elements of the quotation.

Once a supplier has been selected and an order placed, a purchase agreement should be drawn up. The BIC can help on this, but see Units 13 and 14 for details on payment terms and the major forms of documentation raised by the supplier. The purchase agreement should take into account any quality control or inspection procedures and the right to reject goods not conforming to specification. Freight forwarders can handle transportation, storage, documentation, insurance and the complexities of customs entry for the importing firm. They vary in size, services and territories covered – select them with care.

Distributing goods for overseas principals

Firms may choose to purchase the rights to distribute products on behalf of overseas principals. They may: (1) complement existing lines; (2) fill a gap within an existing range; (3) help provide more choice for existing customers. The principles of management, motivation and control, covered in Unit 12, are critical in the establishing of sound distributor/principal relations.

Licensing and cross-licensing

International markets provide a rich source of products, ideas, concepts and expertise which may be available to licence. A prospective licensee can buy or lease the rights to use/manufacture:

1. Overseas patents.
2. Trade marks, trade names, emblems.
3. Toolings/moulds.
4. Designs/drawings.
5. Products/processes.

In return, a royalty payment (usually between 2% and 10% of the firm's selling price) is made. The value of the licence depends on a number of variables, but prospective licensees should consider:

- The size of the potential market for the product/process.
- Its degree of uniqueness.
- The size of territory under offer for licence.
- The degree of protection afforded by patents.
- The degree of exclusivity.

Assistance to be provided at the licensor's cost should be clearly defined within the licence agreement and may include: (1) design services; (2) marketing assistance, particularly in the early days; (3) procurement services and spares recommendations training. Where firms operate in areas of compatible technology, licences can be exchanged on a quid pro quo basis rather than for financial consideration. Opportunities to license or distribute are circulated through the networks (see below: 'What can the BOTB do for me? – the EIS' page 118; and 'Chambers of commerce and industry, page 135), but Tuesday's page of the *Financial Times* offers some exciting prospects (see Figure 5).

Summary

International purchasing and licensing offer many opportunities for the smaller firm to strengthen its domestic trading position. They constitute a natural complement to any exporting activities the firm may be involved in.

Figure 5

Financial Times Tuesday January 29 1985

Business Opportunities

BUSINESS IN ITALY?
Assistance in setting up offices, founding of companies, search of qualified contracts, actions for bad credits, fiscal problems. Apply to:

Box F5424, Financial Times
10 Cannon St, London EC4P 4BY

SPANISH SPECIALITY CHEMICAL FIRM
Basic in polymer chemistry, strongly export oriented with excellent R + D, plant and warehouse facilities and Latin American subsidiary companies, is looking for ways to expand its business activities in the Common Market countries and other areas through agents, distributors, etc.
If interested, please contact:
Box F5462, Financial Times
10 Cannon Street, London EC4P 4BY

SWEDISH MANUFACTURING COMPANY
U.S.A. owned company with 46 years operations in defence and industrial textile fabrication business, seeks partner in support of expansion programmes. Modern factory 100 kms from Stockholm. Employs 60 people. All proposals considered.
Write Box F5457, Financial Times, 10 Cannon Street, London EC4P 4BY

Action Guidelines

1 Are you fully satisfied with existing sources of supply?
___
___
___
___
___
___

2 Which areas cause you real concern?
___
___
___
___
___
___
___

3 Have you considered sourcing from overseas markets?
___
___
___
___
___
___
___

4 Are your competitors sourcing from overseas markets?
___
___
___
___
___

5   Has the firm the time and skills to become involved in importing?

6   How will the firm compensate for currency fluctuations?

7   Has the firm considered licensing:
    - Overseas patents?
    - Trade marks?
    - Toolings/moulds?
    - Products/processes?
    - Designs/drawings?
8   Are there any opportunities for cross-licensing?

3
The Export Experience Base

- Careful analysis of past export experience can provide real clues of export potential.
- Don't cover up past failures in exports. Try to learn from mistakes.
- Experience in managing UK sales agents and distributors is relevant overseas.

Introduction and aims

It is too easy to ignore export experience: it is too simplistic to split smaller firms into non-exporters and exporters, or those with experience and those without. A better division is by level of export experience versus top management's commitment or dynamism (see Figure 6).

1 The non-exporter No commitment to exports and no experience to build on. In reality, this is a fairly small group – mostly recent business start-ups, too involved with surviving in the local domestic market to get involved in exports and too young to gain the interest of overseas buyers.

David, a recent graduate, has bought a fish farm. He intends to process and gift-pack salmon and trout. He believes there is

41

export potential in places like the USA but is concerned with 'getting by' and establishing himself locally.

COMMITMENT

		Low	High
Experience	None	1 Non-exporter	3 Export start-ups
	Some	2 Passive	4 Active

Figure 6

2 The passive exporter No commitment to developing exports, but some historic experience of supplying goods and services overseas, usually via indirect channels such as UK buying houses, or large UK-based customers who in turn export.

A West Midlands designer and manufacturer of clay presses regularly supplied a UK-based customer on an ex-works basis who in turn re-exported the products all over the world.

Invariably the passive exporters are approached direct, but despite these contacts and experience, levels of export commitment and 'dynamism' within the firm remain unchanged.

3 The start-up exporter No export experience but a commitment by top management to investigate export opportunities and invest some management time and effort.

A Yorkshire-based manufacturer and installer of swimming-pool covers instinctively turned to exports when cuts in local authority spending disrupted the growth of its domestic business.

4 Active exporters Firms actively engaged in searching out export business and who view exporting as a mainstream activity.

> A West Midlands firm that designs, manufactures and installs industrial furnaces could not rely on the slow rate of UK investment in new plant, and has built up an operation which seeks to match its resources with international opportunities.

Even non-exporters have categories of experience which may be useful in the export effort. Members of the firm may have experience in foreign travel and languages. More importantly, members of the firm may have experience of working or living overseas, or past business dealings with overseas customers.

> A small company in the South-east, manufacturing equestrian equipment, was considering for the first time exhibiting its products in West Germany. The firm was advised that many exhibition visitors would not speak English, and an interpreter was essential. The managing director almost overlooked the fact that his factory supervisor was of German origin, could assist on the stand and have far superior product knowledge than any contracted interpreter.

Past inquiries

The passive exporting group is probably the largest. Most small concerns will find that they have built up some export experience without making any real commitment. A look through the miscellaneous market file or the general correspondence file will reveal a whole batch of overseas letters and inquiries. This data is an invaluable guide to the company's ability to service export business successfully. The data will take several forms:

- *Letter, telex inquiries*
  Requests for quotations
  Requests to tender
  Requests for samples

> Requests for overseas agency
> Orders
> - *Details of visits, telephone calls*
> Visitors' book
> Exhibition visitors' book

Regular orders from one or a few sources can be a valuable guide to the potential market opportunities. Every success must be followed by the questions:

1 'Why did they contact me?'
2 'How did we win the order?'
3 'What is so special about our business and our capability?'
4 'What customer needs are we meeting?'

Even more important, every failure to win an order or get repeat business must be followed by the same line of questioning. Very often the first consignment for a market can go badly wrong – usually due to a fault in documentation or slow payment. The passive exporter does not have the commitment to learn from this experience.

> A West Midlands drop-forger received a telephone inquiry from Eire. A sample order was dispatched but due to a hold-up at customs the order was late arriving, and extra carriage costs were incurred. The firm 'washed its hands' of the whole affair and did not attempt to win further business in Eire.
>
> A northern furniture upholsterer sent its first sample order to France using in-house transport. It failed to take into account continental bridge clearances and the van crashed into the first low bridge. Since that débâcle, exporting has become a dirty word within the company, tarring the real export potential of the products on offer.

This attitude is typical of many passive exporters where past failures militate against new ventures and change.

Experience of managing intermediaries

Firms exporting, particularly when starting off their exports, frequently deal through agents, export houses, distributors or one of the many different kinds of intermediary that link the firm with end customers. Experience of managing intermediaries in the UK is valuable, as decisions about intermediaries are some of the most complex facing the exporter. This is in part due to the fact that dealings with overseas intermediaries involve long-term commitments and, often, legal obligations. Secondly, it requires the ability to devolve some control and cooperate with an outside organization with different business aims to your own.

> A Darlington-based manufacturer of coal- and log-effect gas fires operates a UK network of nine distributors, each with its own exclusive sales territory. This provided a blueprint for entering European export markets and a body of experience in the complex process of managing distributors.

Competitors' experience

For those firms with a little export experience, analysis may be better directed at the activities of competitors. Are they exporting? Which countries are they exporting to? Useful sources of information may be the trade press and – since firms like to publicize export successes – annual accounts. Although it is no longer a legal requirement, export sales are often detailed separately in the accounts; the chairman's commentary may provide useful indicators.

Summary

Looking inside the business to tap export experience, even for non-exporters, may provide guidelines for follow-up and action. Don't hide past export skeletons in the cupboard; they are indicators of the firm's ability to tackle export markets and of what parts of the business require improvement to meet the challenges of export markets. The export experience base takes a number of forms:

- Experience of working and living overseas.
- Employees' experience of working and living overseas.
- Employees' experience of working in organizations that export or have dealings overseas.
- Experience of handling inquiries from overseas.
- Experience of winning or failing to win business overseas.

Action Guidelines

1. Do members of the firm have experience of foreign travel?

   Substantial ☐
   Some ☐
   Little or none ☐

   Details: _____
   _____
   _____

2. Do any members of the firm have experience of working or living in other countries?

   Substantial ☐
   Some ☐
   Little or none ☐

   Details: _____
   _____
   _____

3. Do any members of the firm speak any languages well?

   Yes ☐
   No ☐

   Details: _____
   _____
   _____

4. Where is the firm located on the experience/commitment matrix?

		COMMITMENT	
		Low	High
EXPERIENCE	None	☐	☐
	Some	☐	☐

5. Do any members of the firm have experience of business dealings abroad?

   Substantial ☐
   Some ☐
   Very little ☐

Details: _____
_____
_____

6 Now collect all the relevant data covering past export experience. Has the firm received export inquiries?

Yes ☐
No ☐

Customer	Market	Date	Details of inquiry
_____	_____	_____	_____
_____	_____	_____	_____
_____	_____	_____	_____

7 Has the firm exported before?

Yes ☐
No ☐

Customer	Market	Date	Details of order
_____	_____	_____	_____
_____	_____	_____	_____
_____	_____	_____	_____

8 Did the firm actively search out the orders?

Yes ☐
No ☐

Details: _____
_____
_____

9 Has the firm had follow-up orders/inquiries from the same source?

Yes ☐
No ☐

Why is this? _____
_____
_____
_____

10 Is the trend of export sales/inquiries:

- up? ☐
- about the same? ☐
- down? ☐

Why is this? _____
_____
_____

11 Does the firm have experience of dealing through intermediaries?

Yes ☐
No ☐

Details: _____
_____
_____

12 Are domestic competitors exporting?

Yes ☐
No ☐

Competitor	*Export country*	*Export sales*
_____	_____	_____
_____	_____	_____
_____	_____	_____

13 What conclusions can be drawn from these action guidelines?
_____
_____
_____
_____
_____
_____
_____
_____
_____
_____

4
Your Commitment: the Key Resource

- Smaller firms have many advantages in servicing overseas customers. Commitment translates this into practical reality.
- Commitment requires careful thought and is based on spending time, money and effort and not just words.
- Commitment is the trigger to export success.

Introduction and aims

Any new development needs a number of things. The aim here is to explore the key resource: your commitment and personal interest in exports. Without a high level of interest from the owner-manager/chief executive it will be difficult to mobilize company resources and win export business.

Think positive

Developing export markets is a long, hard process and it is important that attitudes should be positive from the outset. Firstly, get rid of any misconceptions that export is just for the larger concerns. Over half of the winners of the Queen's Award to Industry for Exports come from smaller firms. Smaller firms take many advantages with them into export markets that larger firms cannot match:

- No complicated levels of management. More rapid decision-making and more flexible responses are possible.
- In an owner-managed company the owner *is* the company and can fully represent the company when overseas.
- More flexible manufacturing and servicing. Hence the ability to supply 'specials', small batches, samples, etc.
- The ability to provide export customers with the personal touch and distinctive service levels.

These at least are some of the theoretical advantages of size which small firms enjoy. Don't be intimidated into thinking that the sheer weight of resources the big firms can throw into export markets gives them all the advantages. Large firms suffer real disadvantages when dealing with overseas customers:

- Bureaucratic inertia, leading to a lack of responsiveness to customers.
- Frequent management changes, creating uncertainty among customers.
- An unwillingness to provide non-standard products and services.

Owner-managers ought to be excited and motivated by the prospect of winning new business from overseas. It should not, however, clash with personal aims and objectives: if travel has no appeal to you and you have no interest in different environments, languages and cultures, then it might be wise to rethink exports. Don't be put off by the apparent complexity of selling overseas – currency movements, hidden tariff barriers, political instability, lack of information about prospective customers, excessive documentation, problems of credit control, etc. There are many agencies, support services and advisory bodies that can help you navigate around these barriers. This book will help locate them and indicate how to use them effectively.

Exports should not be viewed as an easy solution to problems within the domestic market. However, a firm which is successful at home has the potential to repeat that success by moving into international markets. A healthy home market is a sound base from which to grow into export markets. At the same time success in exports can strengthen a firm's domestic business.

Getting started

At a recent Pro-Am golf tournament one of the amateurs asked his professional partner for some guidance. He explained that as he addressed the golf ball on the driving tee there were many thoughts going through his mind: 'Am I keeping my head still? Are my feet correctly positioned? When should I cock my wrist?' – so many, in fact, that he had problems actually commencing the swing. In many ways this is how the aspiring exporter feels; there are so many variables, so much advice and guidance, so many markets to consider, that the firm can be frozen into inactivity. It is the start, 'getting the show on the road', that is the difficult part. The professional golfer advised his partner to apply a small amount of pressure with his left thumb on the club and use this as a 'trigger mechanism' for the rest of the swing. The 'trigger' in the search for export opportunities is making the *commitment* to examine all the key aspects of exporting. Having gathered all the facts to make a decision, *act* (see Figure 7).

This initial commitment will cost (1) time, (2) money and (3) top management effort.

The owner-manager of a successful small North-east metal-spinning company with some experience of exporting made a firm commitment to develop this side of his business. He did this by:

- Joining an export training programme with his finance director and investing eighteen top management days.
- Earmarking £20,000 for export development work to cover travel to Europe and exhibition costs.

Not all small firms can go this far, or will want to go this far. But remember how much time, money and effort was invested in the last successful initiative? Compare it with the last item of capital equipment purchased. This involved analysing the options, deciding what the equipment could do for the business, discussing with other managers. All of these areas involved effort as well as costs, but matching these to the risks of the project and the long-term pay-offs led to action.

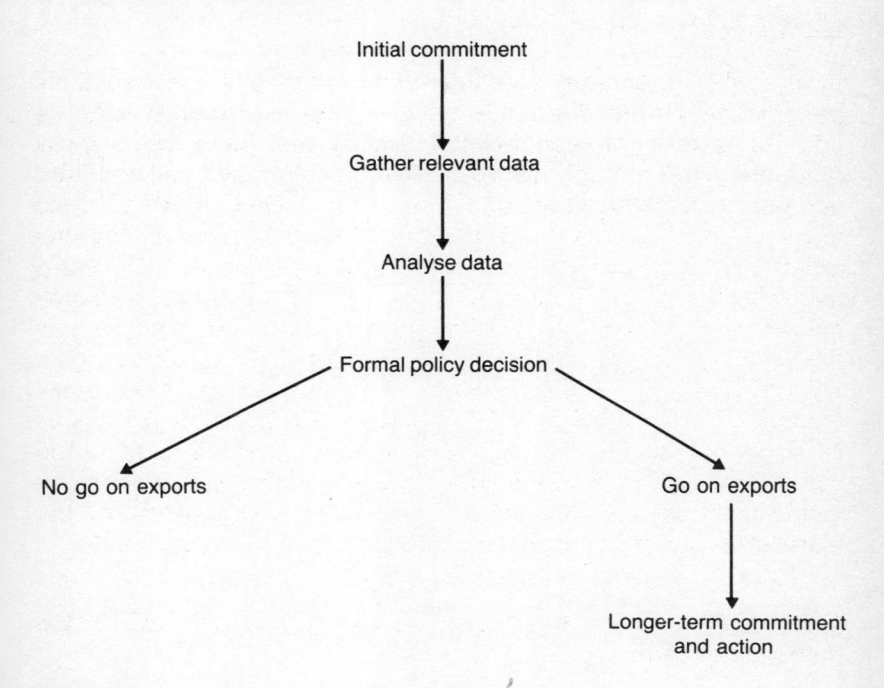

```
              Initial commitment
                     ↓
              Gather relevant data
                     ↓
                Analyse data
                     ↓
              Formal policy decision
              ↙                    ↘
No go on exports              Go on exports
                                     ↓
                              Longer-term commitment
                                   and action
```

Figure 7

Making the time available Sufficient time needs to be allocated in the early stages to:

- Involve all members of the firm in the export initiative. Sell the idea to staff and colleagues. Use it to motivate and build up morale.
- Involve key advisors. The earlier they know about plans the better.
- Develop initial plans and objectives. Assess the likely effects

> of this move on the structure of the business.
> - Measure export potential.

Managers ought to realize that exports, particularly foreign sales trips, will mean being away from the plant for long periods of time. A structured system of delegated authority is an important part of the export effort.

Reasoned commitment It is very difficult to take on commitment to a course of action when risks and pay-offs are unclear. Most firms look to exports to increase profits, but this requires further analysis and reasoning.

> A Yorkshire-based manufacture of welded cans, aerosol valve venting caps and bicycle accessories found that UK sales peaked during June and July, and plant was operating at 70% below maximum capacity. Exports provided an opportunity to (1) utilize unused capacity, (2) reduce unit costs and (3) synchronize fluctuations in sales and production schedules.
>
> A Northern-based manufacturer of protective coverings found that the domestic market had deteriorated due to a price-cutting war between the manufacturers, aggravated by the sluggish UK economy. The owner-manager looked to exports to (1) offset lack of growth in the domestic market and (2) reduce dependence on the domestic market.
>
> A North-east steel stockholder established from industry trends that a South-east competitor was achieving substantial sales in Europe. Although the firm was already exporting to less developed countries, this information provided the spur to analyse the firm's own export potential in Europe. The company looked to new export markets *because competitors were exporting.*

Moves towards exports must sit comfortably with personal objectives and ambitions, such as a desire for prestige or a desire to travel.

> Rockhurst Design Services of Middlesbrough are manufacturers of reaction vessels (autoclaves) and providers of design and manufacturing services for ancillary equipment used in reactor installation. The owner-manager looked to export markets to:
>
> 1. Improve the profitability of the firm.
> 2. Increase the overall sales volume, thus contributing to the company's general expansion.
> 3. Use more fully the management's considerable technological expertise and experience.
> 4. Synchronize seasonal fluctuations in domestic sales.
> 5. Utilize production capacity.

Reasoned commitment is equally applicable to the active exporters whose export department operates on a shoestring, are undermanned compared to the UK sales force and have no representation on the main board. A recent survey found that there was a massive mismatch in the number of personnel employed in the home market compared to the export market (see Table 1).

Table 1

Deployment of sales force in home and export operations – for every five personnel employed in exports

	Exports	*Home market*
West Germany	5	6.2
France	5	8.7
UK	5	29.0

Source: Barclays International Report: *Factors in International Success* (1980).

Top management commitment within active exporting companies should be reviewed to ensure resources are properly balanced between opportunities in exports and the domestic market, and that the full potential of the business is properly developed.

Dorada Wicksteed Ltd, part of the larger Dorada Engineering Group, is a small subsidiary employing 160. It is most famous for its metal and wooden playground equipment, which can be seen on countless local authority playing areas. It also manufactures landscape furniture, associated leisure products and tube expanders. Some 5% of its £5m turnover is sold to export markets. Exporting had taken a back seat within the overall business and had generally been treated in an impassive way, with just one person responsible for order processing and shipping/documentation, and senior management visiting export markets in an *ad hoc* fashion. International competition, problems in controlling overseas agents and high freight rates for the firm's high 'cube' products had further dented confidence and commitment. A newly appointed managing director, Mike Fox, established that increased exports could (1) improve the profitability of Wicksteed, (2) reduce dependence on the declining spending power of the UK local authorities and (3) increase the return on capital invested. He designated exports a key development area. This involved spending a considerable amount of his personal time:

- In getting exports established as an 'integral part of the business and pursued in a positive and meaningful way'.
- Visiting existing agents and customers and establishing common reporting procedures and sales targets.
- Planning to double turnover in twelve months.
- Updating company systems to service efficiently the requirements of overseas markets.

Summary

There are many misconceptions about exporting which may prevent smaller firms from taking the first steps. But export markets provide an opportunity for growth and increased profit which many smaller firms have capitalized upon. Commitment by firms as personified by the top executive has been identified repeatedly as a crucial factor in taking the first steps to successful exporting. The chief executive's involvement will motivate other members of the firm, building up morale and reassuring them of the importance of their efforts. In dealing with foreign buyers or agents the commitment of senior executives demonstrates the substantial nature of the company's export drive.

Commitment to exports requires underpinning by a careful consideration of the firm's specific development interests. Perhaps one of the most dangerous statements put about is that 'exporting is fun'. To approach export markets in a light-hearted, semi-serious fashion may lead to disaster. Established exporting companies pay lip-service to the importance of exports but often lack top management commitment which starves the export effort of the backing and resources required to compete effectively overseas. Top management commitment requires regular reappraisal in the light of the changing opportunities open to the firm.

Action Guidelines

1. Are you willing to respond rapidly to overseas customer requirements on design, product modification, service and price?

   Yes ☐
   No ☐

   If yes, provide details:
   _____
   _____
   _____
   _____
   _____
   _____
   _____

2. Are you willing to provide small specialized production runs for overseas customers?

   Yes ☐
   No ☐

   If yes, quantify service levels:
   _____
   _____
   _____
   _____
   _____
   _____
   _____
   _____

3. As the chief executive are you able to represent the firm in the field and take on-the-spot decisions?

   Yes ☐
   No ☐

4   Do you have the enthusiasm and motivation to open up new markets?

    Yes ☐
    No   ☐

5   If yes, is this enthusiasm shared by your business associates/advisers?

    Yes ☐
    No   ☐

6   What effect has any past experience had on attitudes to future export opportunities that may occur?

    Optimistic   ☐
    Little change ☐
    Discouraged   ☐

    Details: _____
    _____
    _____
    _____
    _____
    _____
    _____
    _____
    _____

7   Are you and other members of the firm willing to spend a significant proportion of your time in exports?

    Yes ☐
    No   ☐

    If yes, quantify:
    _____
    _____
    _____
    _____
    _____
    _____
    _____

8   What percentage of your turnover/volume/profits do you plan to come from export markets?

   Year 1   _____
   Year 2   _____
   Year 3   _____

9   Use the following check-list to help underwrite your commitment to exports:

I look to exports for the following reasons	Very important			Less important	
	5	4	3	2	1

   My competitors are exporting
   I enjoy travelling
   To offset lack of growth in domestic market
   To reduce dependence on domestic market
   To help synchronize fluctuations in production and sales
   To generate employment
   To improve profitability
   To reduce costs
   To improve overall return on investment
   To enhance my standing in the community by winning the Queen's Award or MBE
   Other: _____
   _____

10   Detail the four responses with the highest rating.

   1 _____
   2 _____
   3 _____
   4 _____

5
Mobilizing Export Resources

- Export market opportunities are open to the smaller concern as long as they offer distinctive products and services.
- Products and services or capacity to produce to specification are central to the resource base and the export effort.
- Growth via overseas markets requires a sound financial base.
- Analysis of these export resources is not enough: they need to be mobilized effectively and directed at key export opportunities.

Introduction and aims

Resources are needed for any new development, and exports are no exception. Competition in overseas markets will highlight any deficiencies in resources and how effectively they are mobilized. Many managers are so close to their business they overlook their peculiar mix of resources which create real value and distinction in export markets. This section will help you *audit the resource base*, which includes:

1 Products and services.
2 Physical resources such as plant and machinery.
3 Human resources: employees.

4   Systems, e.g. the way resources are organized.
5   Financial resources.

From this resource base you will be able to analyse the strengths and special capabilities your firm takes into export markets, and the weaknesses and gaps which block the export drive.

What can I offer for export?

Products and service, or even the capacity to produce to specification, form the heart of what is on offer and what customers want. But it is highly unlikely the firm will be able simply to export existing domestic products/services. Usually some modification or amendment will be necessary. Market research, which is covered later (Unit 10), will help establish which modifications or amendments are necessary; but before reaching this stage a firm needs to:

- Analyse the product line to reveal features, benefits and adaptability to overseas requirements.
- Concentrate efforts on products and processes with the greatest export potential.

The idea is to place maximum effort behind the firm's greatest assets. This is equally true for firms offering a jobbing capability or service. In this case, firms should concentrate their efforts on a key industry or group of industries, e.g. the chemical industry, or the mining industry. In some cases, the product to promote or the industry to target upon is self-evident and there is no need for detailed analysis. A careful sounding-out process among people in the trade may provide some pointers. For the majority of firms this will provide clues but no obvious opportunities. In these cases, the products or industries should be selected by taking into account the following factors: return, capacity, confidence and potential.

Product/service analysis

The firm's turnover during the previous twelve months should be broken down for each major sub-category of product or industry supplied.

Furniture Company X (by value)		Plastics Company Y (by value)	
Product	%	Industry supplied	%
Sink units	20	Automotive	30
Kitchen drawer units	16	Furniture	17
Wall units	14	Appliances	14
Kitchen planning service	12	Toy	8
Shelving units	10	Construction	8
Others	28	Others	23
	100		100

A firm with its own product, e.g. the furniture firm, by homing in on products in which the firm and its employees have built up experience and expertise, should be able to ensure that the high standards of quality control and deliveries demanded by export customers are met. The process producer can target on key industries where a knowledge of trade practices or where a good reputation in the home market can be exploited. Major products should be reviewed in terms of:

1 Return.
2 Capacity.
3 Confidence.
4 Potential.

Return The firm should evaluate the relative profit earned from specific products or particular industries. Profit here is the firm's own measure of profitability.

Capacity A clear idea of the firm's target exports, 10%, 20%, 30% of capacity, is important. At the same time, capacity to service this demand, if realized, is necessary.

Confidence In most overseas markets, particularly in the developed world, quality control standards are high. Also the cost of retrieving reject products is far greater than in the home market. This loss is both in monetary costs (shipping rejects cost as much as shipping approved products) and in marketing costs. Before promoting a product or selling goods, the firm should be confident that these standards can be met.

Are we confident of our ability to meet orders to the highest quality standards with the minimum production dislocation?
Yes ☐
No ☐

Potential Firms need to understand the principal features of their products and services, their advantages over domestic customers and the benefits they provide. Competitive advantages revealed in the domestic market may be indications of potential overseas. Critical in this analysis is an understanding of the customer-satisfying benefits the firm is able to provide. This may include:

1 Before- and after-sales service.
2 Training and consultancy service.
3 Financial services.
4 Design services.

Analysis of the product service line under these headings may reveal areas of real strength worthy of consideration for export markets. Many smaller firms will find that concentrating efforts on these strengths will play a major role in realizing their export potential. Attempting to export the entire range from the UK catalogue or adopting the maxim of 'We can make anything for anybody' is likely to result in:

- Wasting resources.
- Failing to distinguish real export product prospects from mainstay home products.
- Lack of precision in the sales and marketing effort –particularly in the areas of in-market pricing and marketing research.

- Extra work in building up a full picture of tariffs, customs dues and regulations.
- Difficulties in briefing the British Overseas Trade Board and support services over the precise nature of the firm's offering.
- Difficulties in negotiations with end users or intermediaries over what is on offer.

For firms without a finished product to take overseas, special attention needs to be devoted to other resources, such as (1) plant, (2) technology and (3) production and marketing systems.

Plastic Moulding (Cradley) Ltd of Halesowen is a trade moulder with no final product to sell overseas, as everything is precision injected to customer specification. Factory visits by overseas buyers therefore form a major part of their export selling operation, as their joint managing director, Tony Bagley, explained:

'Whilst continental companies don't expect regular sales visits, they do expect very prompt replies to questions of a commercial and engineering nature. Delays only result in their lack of interest whilst a prompt reply brings dividends. Most multinational companies, before they place business, will seek recommendations from your existing customers. They will seek information on your company structure, accounts, management and general works administration. They will want to visit your plant for assessment purposes, and some will expect to spend several days doing so. One such visit to our plant was split into three units, two people for two days, another three for two days a month later, and finally two senior people for three and a half days. During the final visit, our management team met them only on the first morning, the last afternoon and two working evenings. These gentlemen all had specific areas they wished to cover, and this included a *close appraisal of our internal methods of communication, records, labour relations and our plans for future development*. In many instances, answers were checked by asking the same questions of different personnel, excluding hourly paid employees. Any unwillingness on the part of a company to participate in this open way can lead to a negative attitude by the visitors to you as a potential supplier. Equally, a positive response can be rewarding, and orders are usually raised requiring a pilot batch of production as a trial run. Provided you can overcome all the hurdles, a long-term relationship can be assured.'

For this thermoplastic injection moulder, a different mix of resources was critical in the winning of overseas business, namely:

Plant, machinery, technology, buildings The age, capacity and shot weight of the machines, the range of working materials including acetates, nylons, acrylics, PVC, vinyls and polypropylene; the design and layout of the plant; working conditions including lighting, heating and ventilation; the overall appearance of the plant and offices and the air of efficiency; location of plant and proximity to airports.

Production systems Finishing and inspection procedures; tolerances; quality circles; wastage rates; ability to take on short runs; production planning and control; down-times.

Marketing and distribution systems Delivery service; emergency delivery services; delivery records; order processing; telex communication; quotation service; technical advisory service; customer records; service records.

Personnel systems Work practices; industrial agreements; reward systems; internal communication; teamwork.

An audit of these resources is important for all firms. It is not enough simply to list the resources within the firm; descriptive information should also be provided. For example, under 'physical resources', the information should include:

1 Age/condition.
2 Location.
3 Comparative performance.
4 Level of utilization.
5 Capability.

We have highlighted the fact that the character and drive of the owner-manager/senior manager will play a critical role in the export development process, but it can also create challenges and changes for other members of the firm. It may involve running a night shift, developing new products which involve differing methods of production and new work practices. It may involve, as in the case of Plastic Moulding (Cradley) Ltd, teams of overseas buyers and customers inspecting the plant. These changes, quite naturally, make people feel apprehensive as they are taken out of their normal routine. It is important that employees are prepared for the changes which entry into export markets brings: (1) *inform* them of export plans, and ask for (2) *feedback*:

- How do they think this will affect their work?
- What impact will it have on the systems within the firm?
- Most importantly, how can *we* as a team respond to the challenges of overseas markets?

Exporting is essentially a team effort. If just one person in the packing department is putting export orders to the bottom of the pile because it involves extra work, then this disrupts the whole firm's efforts. During the 1970s the British Overseas Trade Board ran a campaign called Export United, encouraging greater teamwork and communication within exporting firms. A harmonious, committed and informed work force enthused by management dynamism is one of the most valuable resources the firm can take into exports.

Financial resources for exports

Moves into export markets, like any other developments, incur development costs. It is important that funds are specifically set aside to develop export markets – it cannot be done for nothing (although this book will signpost methods and subsidies to reduce costs). These funds should ensure that a reasonable amount of time is given to the venture and that the plug is not immediately pulled because of a lack of results. The financial director or chief financial adviser should be fully briefed and committed to the venture. He or she should be aware of the financial impact export business can have on the existing business, including:

- The impact of overseas orders on working capital requirements (requirements for pre-shipment finance).
- The impact of debtors on cash flow (payment terms may well be extended for exports).

- Tying up stock and 'specials' for exports.
- The direct costs of additional units.
- The changes in overheads as a result of additional volume.

Analyzing strengths and weaknesses

From an audit of resources, Wickstead Leisure was able to list its specific strengths, which shaped its strategic approach to export markets:

Strengths

1. Systems able to respond to large volume orders.
2. Long established in the UK.
3. In-house design capability.
4. Top management commitment.
5. Catalogue suitable for overseas.
6. Executive quality control.
7. Strong BSI (British Standards Institution) standard awareness.
8. Strong financial background.
9. Modern premises/warehouses.
10. Installation/layout service.
11. Free annual inspection.
12. Excellent delivery record.
13. Wide product range.
14. Extensive exhibition experience.
15. Research and development programme.

Weaknesses, in terms of flexible pricing policies, in-house communication problems and outdated designs of metal equipment, were seen as barriers to export market development.

Summary

Exporting requires a resource base which needs to be realized.

This is made up of:

1 Products and services.
2 Physical resources.
3 Human resources.
4 Systems.
5 Financial resources.

Products and services are the corner-stone of the resource base. They need to be analyzed and reviewed in terms of:

1 Return.
2 Capacity.
3 Confidence.
4 Potential.

For firms without an end product, special analysis is required of the physical and human resources within the firm and the systems which activate these resources. All firms need adequate finance and an understanding of the pressures export business can exert on the financial structure of the company. The resource base of the company needs to be fully mobilized. Very often inadequate and outdated systems prevent effective mobilization. A clear understanding of the resources within the organization highlights strengths which can be capitalized upon when communicating with overseas customers, as well as gaps which require management attention and remedial action.

Product	Turnover % by value	Return	Capability	Confidence	Potential	Total

Turnover   The percentage of the firm's turnover during the last twelve months

Return   Profitability for each product line rated along a ten-point scale:
1.0 ———— 0.1
Excellent profits   Unprofitable
These should be judged individually by product, hence more than one product could be rated a 'good profits' = .7

Capacity   The capacity available for each product is evaluated along a ten-point scale:
1.0 ———— 0.1
Abundant capacity   No capacity

Confidence   The confidence which the firm feels it can vest in product quality maintaining the highest standards demanded by export customers without production dislocation are rated along a ten-point scale:
1.0 ———— 0.1
Completely confident   Unsure

This assumes that the product is priced to satisfy buyer needs. It is confident in making the product the customer is willing to pay for that is important here.

Potential   Perceived potential is rated along a ten-point scale:
1.0 ———— 0.1
Tremendous potential   Very little

These answers should be inserted in the matrix

Industry	% (by value)	Return	Capability	Confidence	Potential	Total

Turnover   The percentage of the firm's turnover being taken up by a consuming industry.

Profitability   Profitability for each industry rated along a ten-point scale:
1.0 ——————— 0.1
Excellent profits   Unprofitable
The overall profitability of business with the industry should be judged rather than specific projects.

Capacity   The amount of capacity available for the types of goods required by each consuming industry is rated along a ten-point scale:
1.0 ——————— 0.1
Abundant capacity   No capacity

Confidence   The confidence which the firm feels it can vest in production output maintaining the highest standards without dislocation is rated along a ten-point scale:
1.0 ——————— 0.1
Completely confident   Unsure

Potential   Perceived potential for the output in the industries overseas is rated along a ten-point scale:
1.0 ——————— 0.1
Tremendous potential   Very little potential

These answers should be inserted in the matrix

Figure 9   *Matrix 2. Industry served/production capability evaluation – quantitative audit*

Action Guidelines

1 Complete matrix 1 (Figure 8) or matrix 2 (Figure 9), for example:

Product	Turn-over	Return	Capability	Confidence	Potential	Total
Sink units	20	0.6	0.8	0.8	0.6	
Kitchen drawer units	16	0.5	0.7	0.8	0.7	
Wall units	14					
Kitchen planning service	12					
Shelving units	10					
Others	28					

2 List the products or processes for specific industries with the highest ratings:

1 _____

2 _____

3 _____

4 _____

3 Do your colleagues agree with this ranking?
   Yes ☐
   No ☐

4 What customer needs do these products or processes meet?

_____
_____
_____

5 Do you have advantages over:
   - UK suppliers?
   - foreign competitors?

Specify: _____
_____
_____
_____

6   Audit your range of resources.

	Production	Marketing and distribution	Finance	Personnel	Other
Physical	☐	☐	☐	☐	☐
Human	☐	☐	☐	☐	☐
Systems	☐	☐	☐	☐	☐

7   What gaps exist in your range of resources?
_____
_____
_____
_____

8   How do these resources compare with those of your closest competitors?
_____
_____
_____
_____

9   What are the major strengths you take with you into export markets?
_____
_____
_____
_____
_____
_____

6
Using the Firm's Network

- Effective exporting requires the rational selection of export market opportunities.
- The smaller firm is at the heart of a network of contacts which provides valuable information about export opportunities.
- Tapping this network is the starting point in the market selection process.

Introduction and aims

One of the most complex problems facing the 'start up' exporter is where to direct initial exporting effort. For the existing exporter, the problem takes the form of how to get the most out of existing markets and comparing these markets with other opportunities. At the centre of successful exporting is the selection of those market opportunities where the firm has:

1. Some differential advantage in winning the business.
2. The capability to service the business in the long term.
3. The opportunity for reasonable profits.

Part of the problem is the sheer width of opportunity open to the exporter: more than 149 countries in differing stages of economic development with their own particular social and cultural characteristics. These countries are composed of markets and sub-markets which in turn are made up of individual customers with their differing needs and buying practices. These markets are constantly changing and throwing up fresh opportunities.

Overwhelmed by the complexity of the choices and the problems of plugging into opportunities open to them, many firms simply divide the world into domestic and export business and react to export inquiries on an *ad hoc* basis. Servicing export markets in this arbitrary manner may lead to some export orders, particularly in the non-durable consumer goods area, or for products which do not require long-term commitments to the market, i.e. after-sales servicing, spares, etc. But this approach can lead to a misallocation of valuable management time and provide poor returns.

> A small foundry had done business in over forty countries over the previous five years, but never amounting to more than 3% of capacity. The firm was reluctant to take exporting any further as the amount of time and effort put into servicing this business was far out of proportion to the returns. This is a fairly common situation: large numbers of markets, a great deal of work and relatively small returns for the effort involved.

In such a case, no real expertise is gained on the needs of specific markets, and this deficiency extends into technical specification, packaging, customs duties and the other variables of international trade. Success in export markets depends heavily on a firm's ability to adjust to the requirements of the market, and therefore the selection of markets is a key decision which requires careful analysis and research. The aim of the next two units is to provide the smaller firm with a methodology for selecting markets – markets which will become as much a part of the resource base of the firm as products/services, management, plant, etc.

In the last unit we looked at resources, and perhaps one of the major 'intangible' resources is the firm's network of contacts: these contacts and their degree of usefulness may be stored on the back of an envelope, in a diary or simply in the manager's head. This section attempts to unlock the real contribution this network can make.

Understanding the network

No business operates in isolation, and the network of contacts surrounding the smaller firm can provide important pointers for the selection of export market opportunities. The first stage in the market selection process is to build a clear picture of the firm's network of possible points of contact with export markets. The network will include:

1 Previous business/inquiries.
2 Contacts.
3 External relationships.
4 Export organizations.

(See Figure 10.) Through this network very many smaller firms have access to an enormous range of overseas contacts, volumes of information, massive help and even substantial funds. It can be used to win business.

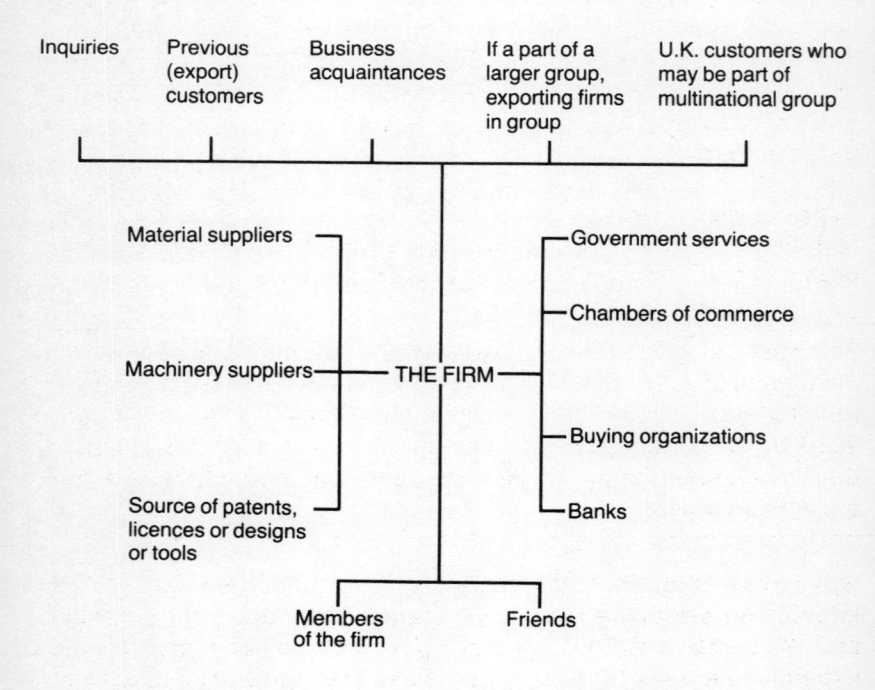

Figure 10 *A firm's network of possible points of contact with export markets*

Effectively managing the network

There are certain principles which need to be stressed before the firm tackles this network.

1 The contact points on the network represent a wide array of valuable resources. Many of the firms and individuals who will be identified can be of tremendous help to the small exporter. However, they are normally independent of the firm with a primary responsibility to themselves or their own firm. Any aid sought should be well thought out and discriminating.

2 Perhaps the most common criticism of smaller firms by the management of larger firms or external organizations is that, even when positive help is provided, action is seldom taken by the smaller company. It would be irresponsible of the managers of small firms to act on proposals or ideas given by outsiders if it is not in their interests. Contacts in South Korea are irrelevant to the firm targeting its efforts on Eire. The general direction of the organization's efforts should be explained. A clear, well-thought-out brief is perhaps the most important part of any information-gathering process.

Tapping past experience This is the starting-off point in any search for new business. Longer-established firms may find export orders dating back into the company's early years.

> The newly appointed managing director of a small mattress manufacturer in the South-east, which was part of a larger group, found a record in the files of a shipment to New York some fifteen years earlier. Nobody in the firm knew details of the customer, or their reaction to the products, and nobody had bothered to ask for a follow-up order.

By sifting through past business, two important pieces of information are being sought: (1) markets with apparent potential and (2) contacts worth approaching. If the company has no past experience in exporting, or export sales are highly limited, consult the sales inquiry file. Has the firm received from overseas:

1 a request for product information/catalogues/samples?

2 a request for a quotation?
3 a request to tender?

Many of these inquiries are discarded or overlooked, but they constitute a wealth of information. For those companies that have no export experience or inquiries, it may be worth examining the export activities of competitors. Where are they exporting? Are they exhibiting overseas?

Contacts These are the life-blood of any small firm and in many ways form a major *intangible* resource. Business acquaintances, members of the firm and friends frequently have at their disposal a large amount of information and advice. In some cases the contacts will be available on a more formal basis. *Many small firms are parts of larger groups.* In some cases the group will have either a central export service or firms in the group with export experience. These services should be tapped where appropriate. However, every firm, even within a group, must set its own goals and targets. A common mistake by small firms in a group is to use the group's agency network without examining whether these agents can handle its product or have the marketing skills to win it business.

Two chemists established a partnership after formulating a specialist feed supplement for goats. They decided to approach their old employer – a large veterinary products company – to help them get established in export markets. The veterinary company helped them win a contract to supply feed supplements to a herd of 4000 goats in Muscat, and they are helping them promote their products in Australia at the Perth Agricultural Show.

External relationships Many UK customers will be part of *multinational* firms, at least in the sense of having associated firms overseas. The annual reports of firms and internal newsletters will normally highlight overseas activities, often including details of the main industries, prospects, locations, even senior executives of overseas firms. Approaches to good customers can frequently generate a surprisingly positive response. One firm, for example, found that it had developed a tool for a multinational customer.

The end product was due to be made throughout the world. Following the supplier's approach, the UK buyer contacted his US counterpart. The result was sole supplier status for the USA as well as Great Britain.

Customer relations may preclude such an approach. However, there is usually less reservation about using *suppliers of machinery* or *materials* as sources of information, advice and contacts. Many UK firms are helpful to smaller firms. This can even extend to introductions to prospective agents and distributors. Overseas suppliers are likely to have considerable in-depth knowledge of their home markets. It is not unusual, though, for them to have some 'down-the-line' involvement making them competitors in that market.

> A Midlands emergency lighting company approached its
> UK battery supplier for information on the French market and was
> astonished at the number of contacts and detail the supplier
> was able and willing to offer.

Many companies hold *licences*, *designs* or *tools* from overseas companies. Normally the contracts governing this type of relationship define the market areas or spheres of activity. Within the firm's accepted operating area the *licensor* may have information and contacts capable of opening markets up to the licensee.

The data gathered so far has been largely informal and unstructured, but has the great advantage of immediacy. There exists a wide array of more formal sources of the necessary background information and potential contacts.

Export organizations

BOTB The British Overseas Trade Board (BOTB) offers a wide array of services, including background information and names of possible contacts (the range of BOTB services is reviewed later in Unit 8). A number of other government departments have shown themselves to be very export orientated. The Department of Health and Social Security has a particularly commendable record of assisting firms supplying medical equipment and associated goods. The array of state services is complemented by other organizations.

Chambers of commerce and industry A frequent criticism about government services is that they are insufficiently specialized to meet the needs of smaller firms. This need for specialized help may be supplied by trade associations. The chambers of commerce and industry have a particularly proud record in this area. The chambers of commerce and industry of the major cities provide help in many areas, ranging from telex through to organizing trade missions. The International Chamber of Commerce encompasses most of the major industrialized and industrializing countries.

Banks Over the last few years, the banks have broadened their range of services to provide much more commercially orientated help. These range from communicating the company's name and interests to overseas branches, and informing them of inquiries, through to providing considerable background information. Ultimately, most of these sources cannot satisfy the prime requirement: *orders*.

A Nottingham-based upholsterer of up-market furniture was about to visit the Netherlands. The firm's bank arranged, via its correspondent bank in Amsterdam, a meeting with the buyer from the largest Dutch retailer of quality furniture, at twenty-four hours' notice.

Buying houses The various types of UK buying houses can place orders. Often they serve to direct potential suppliers to the appropriate buyers overseas.

A careful completion of the 'catalogue of contacts' in the action guidelines provides a starting-off point for the export effort. Some firms will find that a clear picture of likely opportunity areas emerges. For other firms, the range of countries is extremely large and no clear guidance to obvious priorities emerges. At this stage a new problem often replaces the initial areas of difficulty encountered by the firms' 'lack of contacts', 'no market information', 'no experience'. This new problem, 'I have the contacts but just don't have the time to do anything about them', is a much more real and long-term problem.

Summary

By (1) realizing the network of contact points which surround the firm, (2) using this network to help direct export efforts and (3) learning from and capitalizing on past experience, the firm will have some insights into locating export opportunities. These low-cost, home-based activities may provide more meaningful guidelines to future export action than any amount of formalized market research. Using the firm's network is not a 'one-off' activity: maintenance of the contact list and openness to the contribution the network can make are prerequisites for export development.

Action Guidelines

Point of contract	Potential export link	Country contract(s)	Contacts
Materials supplier	Yes/No	_____ (Detail)	_____ (Detail)
Machinery supplier	Yes/No	_____ (Detail)	_____ (Detail)
Sources of patents, licences, designs or tools	Yes/No	_____ (Detail)	_____ (Detail)
Members of firm	Yes/No	_____ (Detail)	_____ (Detail)
Friends	Yes/No	_____ (Detail)	_____ (Detail)

1. Complete the following catalogue of contracts:

		(Detail)	(Detail)
Previous (export) customers	Yes/No		
Business acquaintances	Yes/No		
UK customers part of multinational firms	Yes/No		
Other exporting firms in group	Yes/No		

83

Inquiries	Yes/No	(Detail)	(Detail)
Government services	Yes/No	(Detail)	(Detail)
Chambers of commerce	Yes/No	(Detail)	(Detail)
Buying organizations	Yes/No	(Detail)	(Detail)
Banks	Yes/No	(Detail)	(Detail)

Point of contact	Frequency of contact	Country contact	Contact
		Market opportunity area most frequently mentioned:	Strongest contacts (names)
		1 _____	1 _____
		2 _____	2 _____
		3 _____	3 _____
		4 _____	4 _____
		5 _____	5 _____

2 Now summarize this information:

7
Selecting Export Opportunities

- World markets require systematic screening to eliminate areas with low export potential.
- Countries are composed of various markets and sub-markets. Some of these are composed of potential customers.
- Company resources are more profitably directed at key potential customers.
- Selectivity means saying yes to some opportunities and no to others.

Introduction and aims

There are many ways of looking at markets which expose different kinds of market opportunity: see Figure 11 for a view of the world as we normally see it. But population is often the key to market size: Figure 12 vividly illustrates how poor a guide to markets geography is. However, wealth is frequently far more important for profitability and this is distributed along very different lines (see Figure 13).

Any attempt to establish priorities within these changing market patterns and invest in meaningful concentration requires:

- *Market information*, of a type appropriate to the firm.

> • An approach to organizing information to ensure that the best markets emerge.

Some sources of market information are identified in the ensuing unit. To ensure they are used when appropriate, information sources are identified and related to the different types of market selection approach proposed.

1 Personal priority.
2 Maximizing returns from current activities.
3 Simple eliminiation.

Managers are especially afraid of saying no to what might turn out to be an important opportunity. This anxiety is expressed in the view that 'We might pick the wrong country: it's safer to spread the risk'. The aim of this unit is to reduce the fear of incorrect selection to an acceptable minimum through careful analysis and research.

Personal priority

When the manager has a clear personal preference for specific countries (peoples) this provides the direction for the export effort. This may sound unscientific, but if the manager has some enthusiasm for the culture or point of contact with the market, it provides considerable advantage in the development of the market.

> The owner-manager of a Yorkshire micro-nutrients company regularly holidayed in France, and during his visits gained experience of arable farming methods. He now exports on a regular basis and enjoys his continued contact with the market.

The corollary of this is that, if you don't enjoy the prospect of visiting and selling into particular markets (e.g. Iraq because of the distance, 'culture clash' and dangers due to the conflict with Iran), it is unlikely you will succeed. For the small firm, the determination

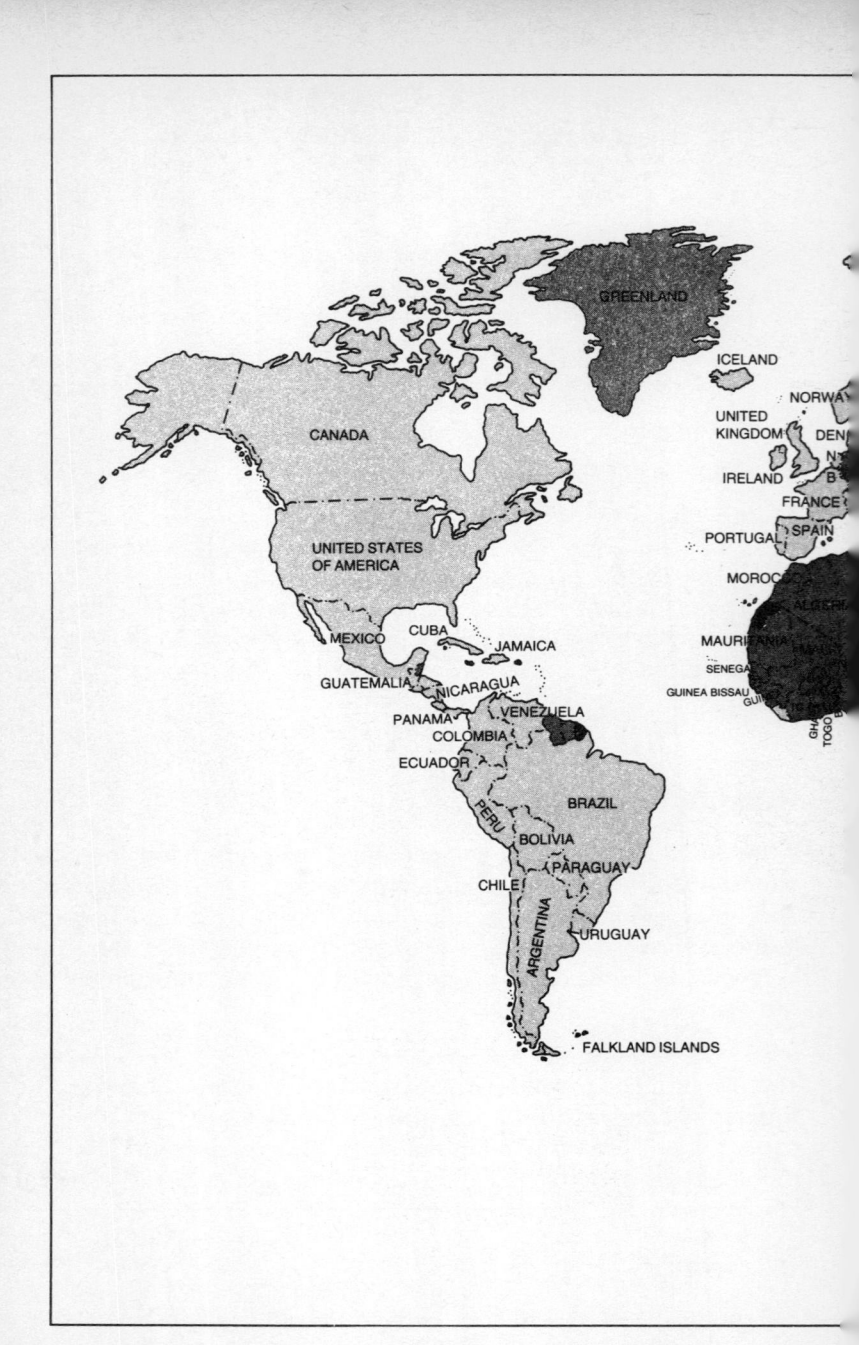

Figure 11

Sovereign states in and since 1945

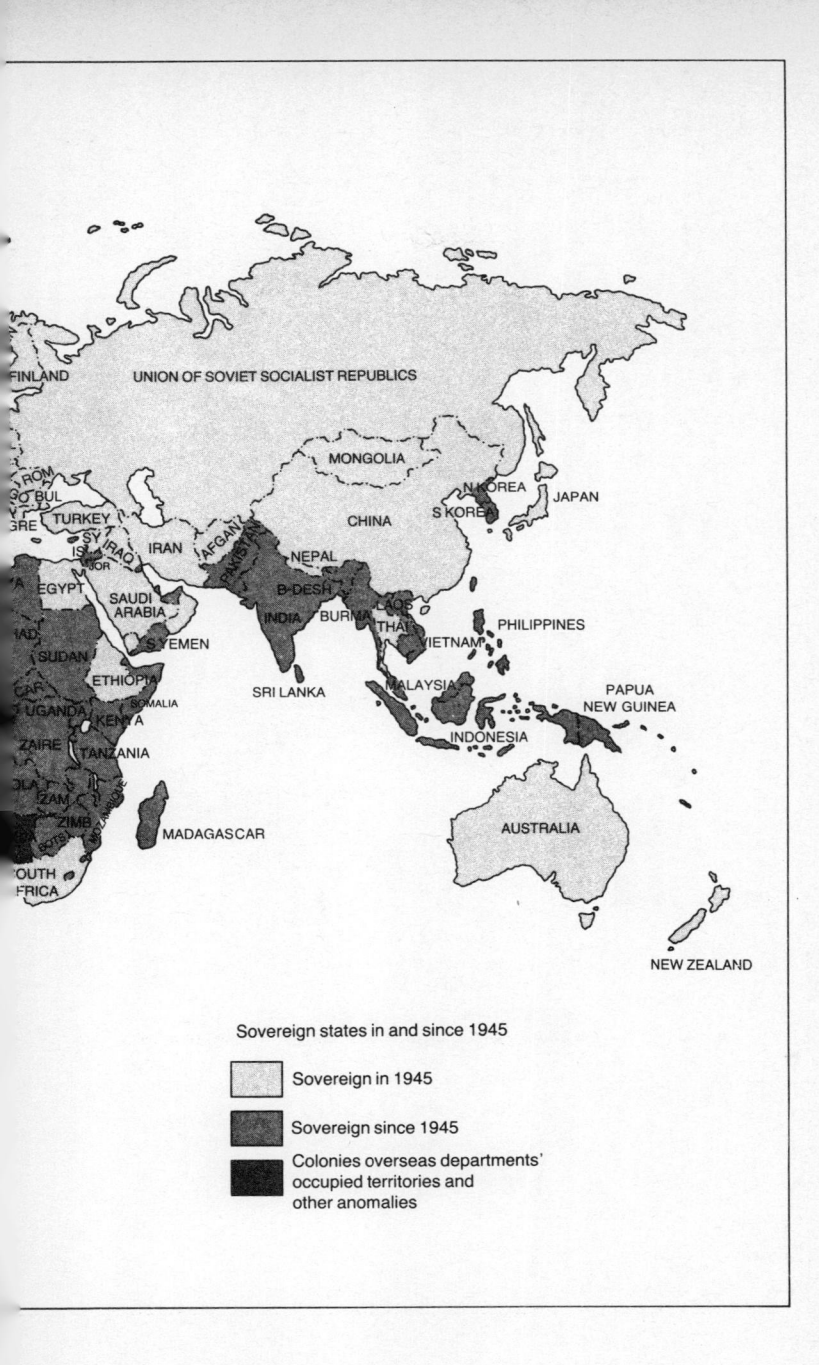

☐ Sovereign in 1945

▨ Sovereign since 1945

■ Colonies overseas departments' occupied territories and other anomalies

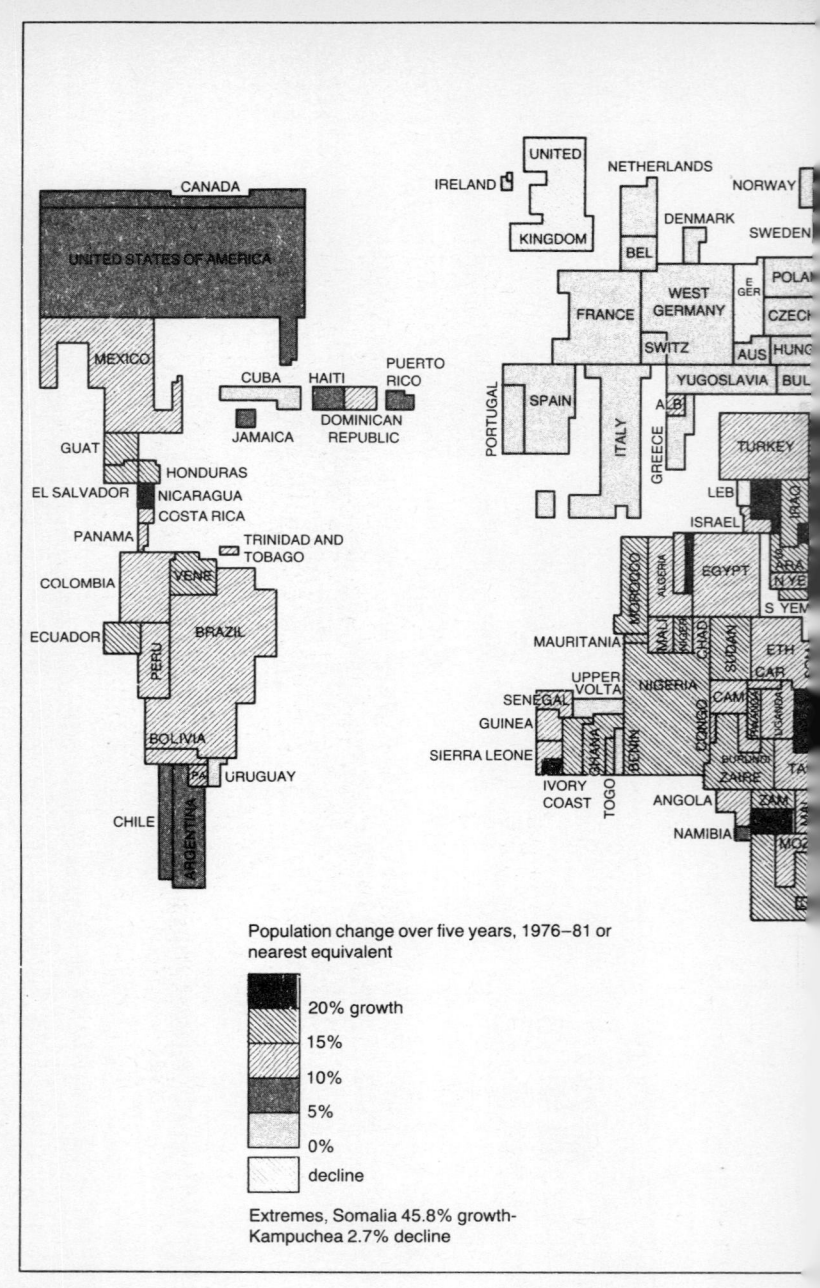

Figure 12

NLAND

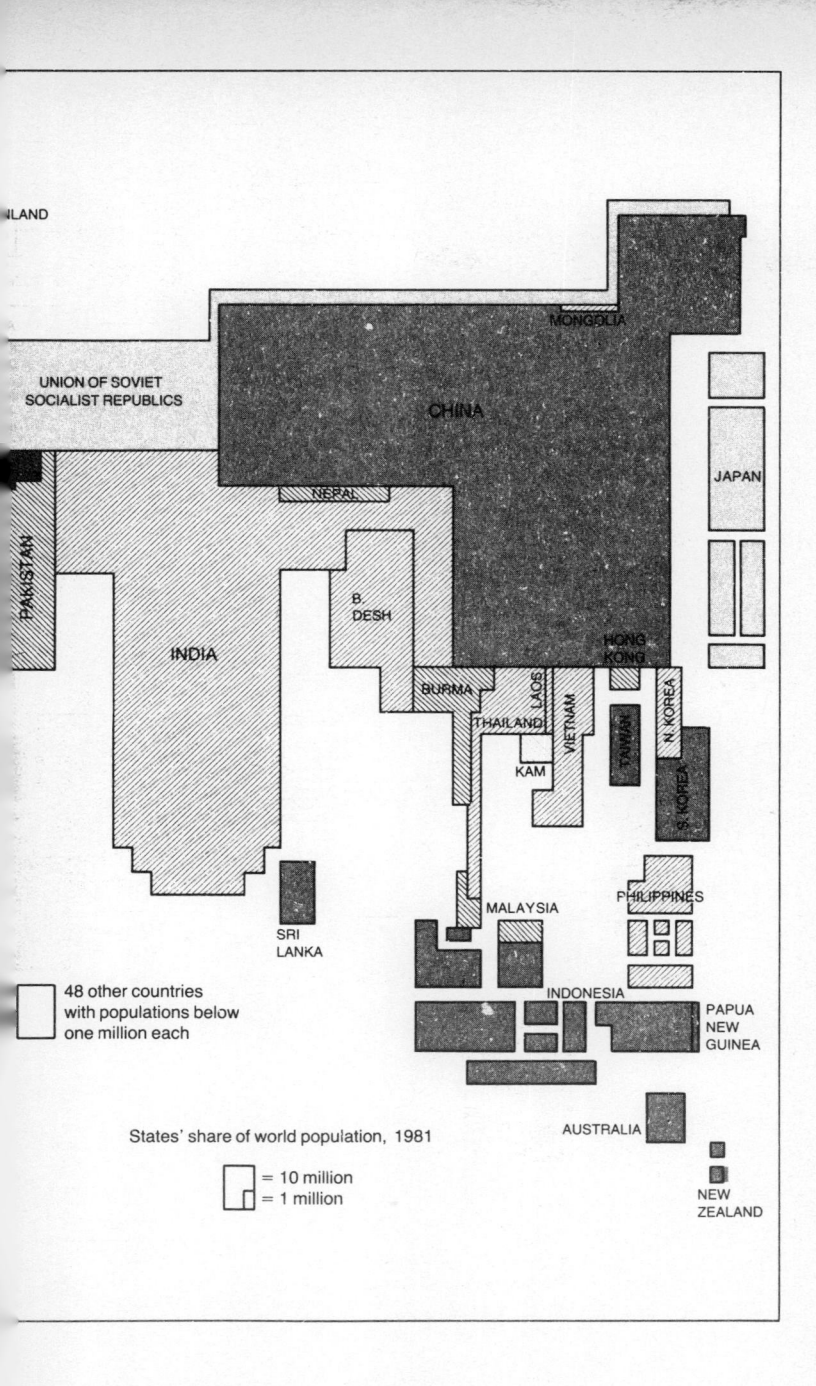

UNION OF SOVIET
SOCIALIST REPUBLICS

MONGOLIA

CHINA

JAPAN

PAKISTAN

NEPAL

B. DESH

INDIA

BURMA

HONG KONG

LAOS

THAILAND

VIETNAM

N. KOREA

KAM

TAIWAN

S. KOREA

SRI LANKA

MALAYSIA

PHILIPPINES

INDONESIA

PAPUA NEW GUINEA

AUSTRALIA

NEW ZEALAND

48 other countries with populations below one million each

States' share of world population, 1981

☐ = 10 million
☐ = 1 million

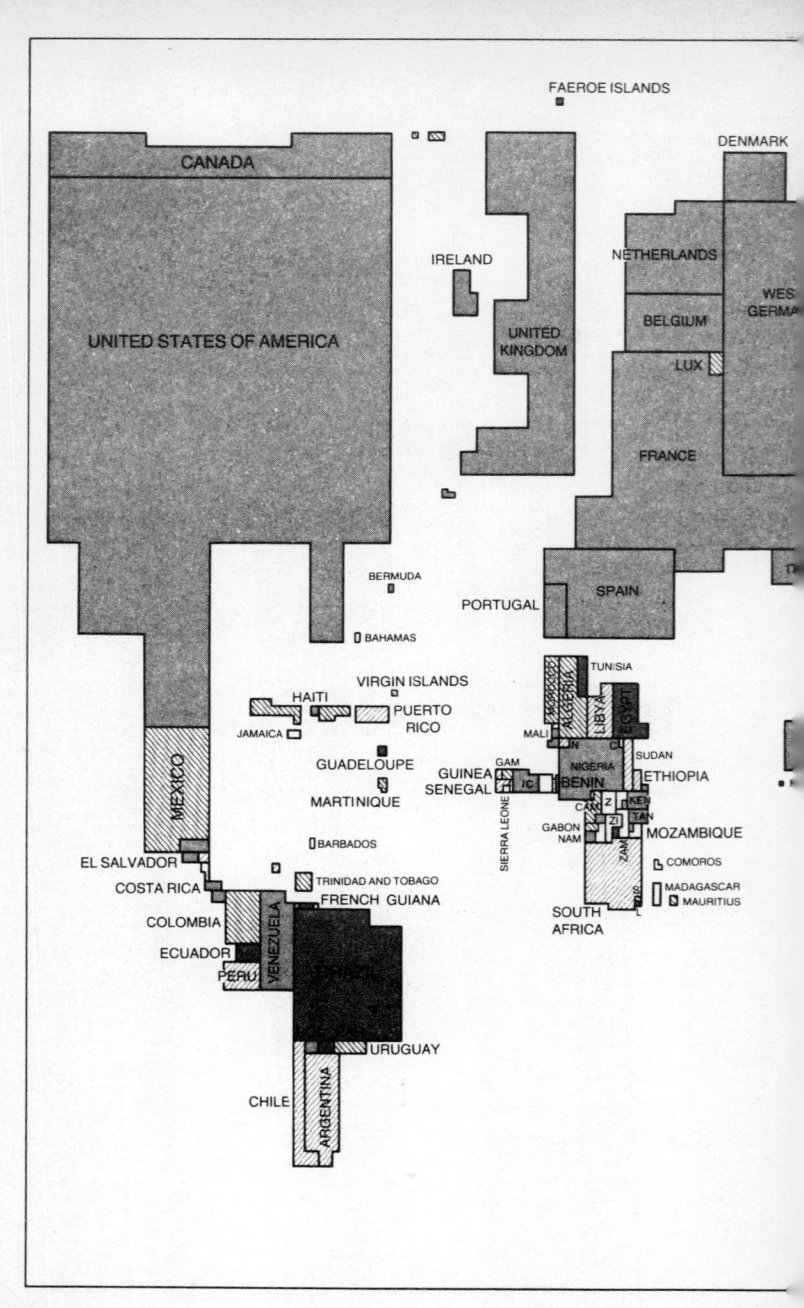

Figure 13

Growth decline in income per head, 1970–80

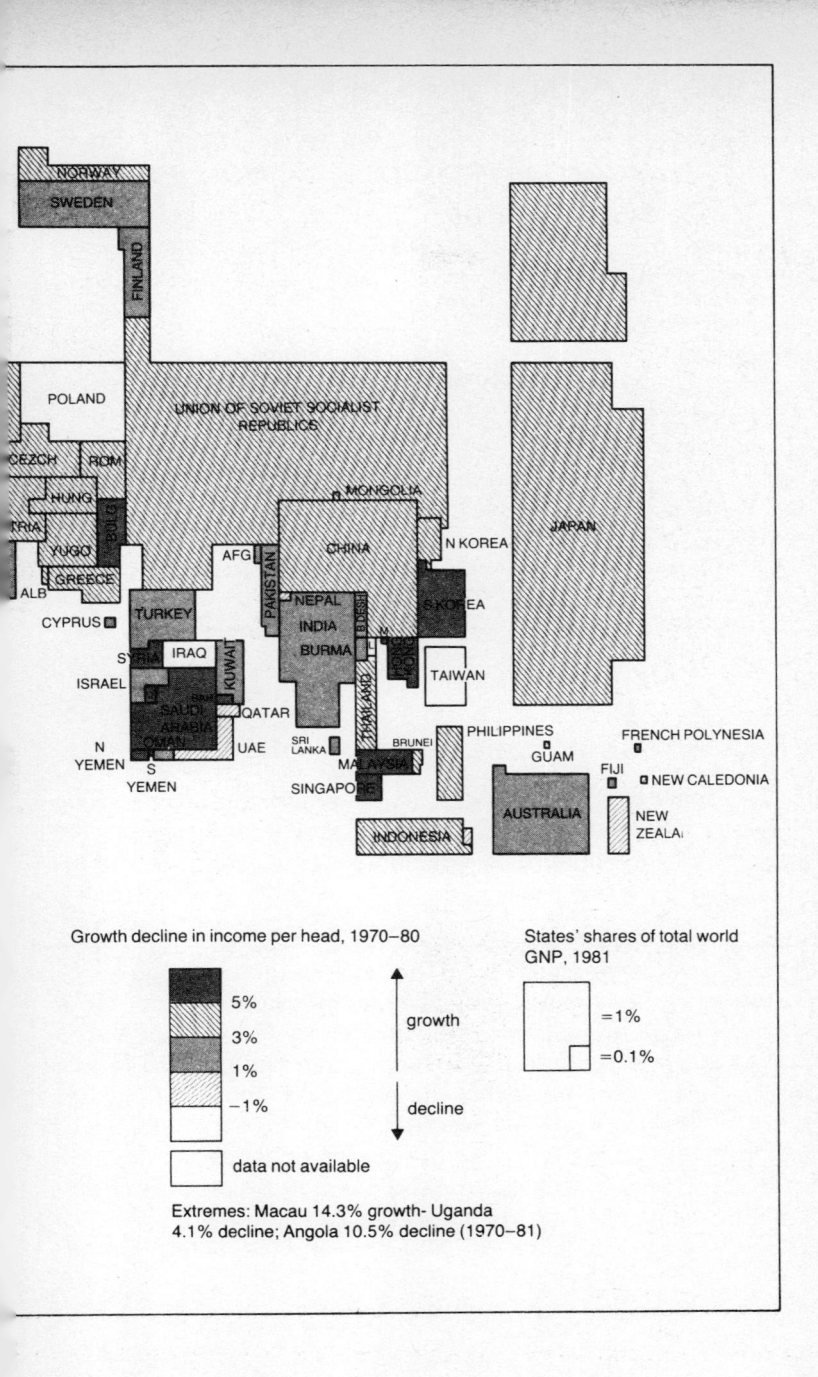

- 5%
- 3%
- 1%
- −1%

growth ↕ decline

data not available

Extremes: Macau 14.3% growth- Uganda 4.1% decline; Angola 10.5% decline (1970–81)

States' shares of total world GNP, 1981

□ =1%
▫ =0.1%

to build up long-term trading relations may well have no surer basis than the desire of top managers to establish or reinforce long-term personal links.

For some firms, the priorities of UK customers dictate which export markets they should service.

> Take Advanced Lubrication Services Ltd of County Durham, which supplies specialized lubricants to the off-shore industry via an office in Aberdeen. The recession in the North Sea oilfields and the development of drilling in the Far East and China have produced demands for local service. Where the rigs are located, ALS and other suppliers must follow. Where down-time on the rigs cost $50,000 a day, an adequate and swift local supply is essential. ASL is now establishing a stock and service centre in Singapore City.

Maximizing returns from existing contacts

A rigorous search through the catalogue of contacts may provide the jumping-off point for future growth. It may sound obvious but many companies overlook their existing export customers and fail to exploit their full order potential.

> Following a chance meeting on holiday, a Nottingham-based distributor of plastic commercial stationery had won an order to supply pocket files to a customer in New South Wales, Australia. Following the initial contact, all communication had been by letter and telex, including the news that the order was 'short-shipped'. Problems of this kind in the UK would normally be handled by an immediate call by the owner to the customer; written communication tended to exacerbate the export problem and created a loss of credibility. The managing director eventually decided to ring the customer – at 2.00 a.m. UK time. The customer was so delighted with this personal attention that a further order for half a million pocket files was placed.
>
> John Mason & Son Ltd of Leek, an established manufacturer of

lingerie and ladies' fashionwear supplying UK chain stores and mail-order houses, was approached direct by a major West German mail-order house on a mission to the UK. 'We were asked to supply a trial order of velour housecoats.' says Mason's director, Mark Jones. 'Six years later the housecoat is our single largest-selling style and they still take the one item.' The account is important to the firm's prosperity. However, it has generally been treated with a trepidation and reserve totally alien to the firm's UK accounts. Service levels were often worse, visits irregular and the entire effort kept divorced from the normal run of home business. The business base grew as calls were arranged in conjunction with Mason's designer. Efforts were made to introduce new lines by careful research and development work on West German tastes and styling. This account now gets the same treatment as any UK key account; business has improved and is more secure, and, what is more, progress has been made in getting new West German accounts.

A small manufacturer of moulded and stamped rubber products, part of the BET group, had a number of European agents who were left to their own devices. Occasional contact was made by letter only. Following a suggestion that communication and motivation could be improved by telephoning agents on a regular basis, the firm found that orders from the West German agent tripled following a business call.

Simple elimination

This process involves eliminating all those countries failing to meet criteria set by the firm to suit its requirements or the capabilities of its relevant personnel. The key categories are:

1 Company-specific factors.
   2 Economic evaluation.
      3 Market conditions.
         4 Competitive evaluation.

These filtering steps will allow the firm to eliminate from further study markets where they have little competitive advantage or which offer little market potential.

Company-specific factors Using the in-company resource check-list and any relevant subjective criteria, the company eliminates all markets failing to satisfy certain conditions. A list of possible criteria for elimination might include:

1. Similar business morality to UK, i.e. no back-handers, bribes, etc.
2. English as an acceptable business language.
3. Ability to be serviced by sales, technical or other staff from UK in 48/72/96 hours.
4. Easy access for goods by sea/road/air from UK.
5. Approximately the same time zone as UK.

Table 2
Using 'English as an acceptable business language' criterion

149 members of the UN	*Eliminate* Comecon, China, Indo-China, France, Spain, Portugal, former French, Spanish and Portuguese possessions, Greece, Turkey, Middle East, South America, Indonesia.
	Leaves Australia, Canada, Benelux, Bangladesh, Eire, India, New Zealand, Pakistan, Scandinavia, USA, West Germany, former British possessions in Africa, Hong Kong, Singapore, Korea, Japan, Taiwan, Malaysia.

Table 2 shows an unmanageable group of 149 countries being reduced to a shorter list of countries with one fundamental factor in common: communication in a common language is possible. The criteria for elimination used earlier can be used singly or in combination: a combination of language and ease of access by sea and road would shorten this list to Canada, USA, West Germany, Benelux and Scandinavia for a foundry on Merseyside.

Information sources These are extensive and freely available at this level. An economic atlas will provide information such as 'acceptable business languages', industries, trading conditions, time zones and even major routes. All prospective exporters should invest in a good atlas (e.g. *The Times Atlas of the World*, Times Books). Details of access to markets, specific routes and means of reaching them can be obtained from freight forwarders, shipping agents and hauliers (road, sea and air). Information on time zones and ease of personal access is normally obtainable from a good travel agent.

Economic evaluation For the vast majority of firms, the list of countries is still far too long. A more substantial examination of the economic conditions of the specific countries or regions is necessary to whittle the list down. For many firms a particular level of economic development or technological structure is necessary for exports to be viable. Economies can be classified and evaluated in terms of a number of different criteria (see list below). Each firm needs to consider seriously the economic forces which led to its previous sucesses and match them against overseas markets.

A small pump manufacturer found that its best export market was for one of its older models of pump. It had been developed for use in wet mining conditions by relatively unsophisticated miners in the first quarter of this century. It was cheap and easy to use. For these reasons it was greatly preferred in less developed countries to its much more 'efficient' rivals, which the miners often found too complex to use and difficult to repair.

Contact point

For information on small industry openings in developing countries and intermediate technology applications in the Third World, contact:

Intermediate Technology Industry Services, Myson House, Railway Terrace, Rugby CV21 3HT (0788 70126).

Possible criteria of economic evaluation are:

1   Advanced developed economies (rich) (see Table 3).

2 Rapidly developing economies (rich).
3 Less developed economies (poor).
4 Mixed economies.
5 State-controlled economies.
6 Economies with high disposable incomes.
7 Economies with rapidly growing populations.
8 Low-skill economies (high levels of illiteracy).
9 High-skill economies (high terminal education ages).
10 Economies with specific industries.

For a firm selling gas appliances, the wide availability and distribution of gas is a basic economic criterion in screening world markets.

**Table 3
Using 'Advanced developed economies' criterion**

149 members of the UN

Stage 1	Stage 2
Company-specific criterion (Table 2) leaves in all the countries where English is the acceptable business language.	*Eliminate* Bangladesh, India, Pakistan, former British African possessions, Korea. *Leaves* Australia, Canada, Benelux, Eire, New Zealand, Scandinavia, USA, West Germany, Singapore, Japan, Taiwan.

Information sources More detailed information now needs to be collected. Some of it, e.g. level of development, may be available from sources used earlier, for example the economic atlases, but these are often out of date, particularly concerning dynamic areas such as economic development (the date/edition needs to be carefully examined). There is a vast fund of information on all these criteria available in central, university and polytechnic libraries. The majority of university and some polytechnic libraries have subject-specialist staff capable of giving skilled guidance on their particular areas. Particularly useful sources of information are United Nations economic surveys, Organization for Economic Cooperation and Development publications, and the publications of specific countries – US statistics are particularly good, (see box for a short list). For details of Britain's trade in specific commodities with particular countries, HM Customs and Excise provide an invaluable source of assistance. Prior to visiting any of these libraries, telephone to check on availability of information and assistance.

Working through these information sources takes time and takes you away from the plant. This work can be subcontracted out to university, polytechnic and college business studies undergraduates whose courses usually incorporate some form of practical project work. Contact the lecturing staff for further information.

The major banks provide a considerable amount of material and information on overall economic performance for specific countries: Abecor, Midland Bank Tradebrief and National Westminster's economic reports are produced regularly and are good sources of background information (see Figure 14). Lloyds Bank Overseas provides a much more detailed and substantial 'economic survey' of particular countries. Lloyds Bank Overseas also produces the invaluable *Economic Report* which lists specific projects. The help and advice of the banks at this level is tremendous.

Figure 14

Midland Bank International

tradebrief

March 1985

Tradebrief is issued monthly and edited by the Publications Unit, Midland Bank International. Enquiries about any items should be made to the London Editor; telephone 01-623 9393 extension 6104 or telex 888401 quoting the edition.

1/Africa

Burundi

Burundi Economic Memorandum, a report by the International Bank for Reconstruction and Development on agriculture, energy, industry, health and education priorities, is available for inspection through the World Aid Section, (or regional offices) British Overseas Trade Board, 1 Victoria Street, London SW1H OET, UK; tel. 215 3911.

Seychelles

A $380m investment programme under the 1985-9 development plan will include tourism, the fishing industry and agriculture. Existing tourist facilities will be improved and new hotels built. Hospital building will double the number of beds. Development of Victoria Port is planned, and water and sewerage services will be improved.

Tanzania

Eight major power projects have been identified in a hydroelectric masterplan for the Rufiji Basin Development Authority. For further information contact: Ministry of Water and Energy, PO Box 9153, Dar es Salaam.

Tunisia

A final feasibility study on setting up a chemicals complex at Zarzis is to be considered by the government, which is

2/Asia

Bangladesh

A project to expand energy supply from the current rate of 430m cubic feet per day to 840m by the end of the Third Five-year Plan in 1989-90, is to be financed by a loan of $103.8m from the Asian Development Bank.

● Development of 3,000-sq km of swampland in the Khulna and Satkhira districts is planned by the Water Development Board, and Ministry of Power and Water (MPW). The Asian Development Bank has approved a technical assistance grant for a feasibility study. Contact: MPW, Extension Building, Dhaka.

China

More than $1bn is expected to be spent during 1985 on imports of new

World Bank. For details contact: Director General, Office of the National Ports of Cameroon, PO Box 4020, Douala.

Congo

A $35.5m programme to upgrade the national and international telephone services has been announced by the Ministry of Information, Posts and Telecommunications. Finance is being arranged with international fund organisations. For details contact the Ministry at: Palais de Peuple, Brazzaville. Telex 5210.

Ghana

Credit of $60m is expected to be agreed soon by the International Development Association for the import of essential products for the agricultural, transport and manufacturing sectors. Repairs and modernisation of bridges, main roads and feeder roads will be financed by a credit of $40m.

Malawi

Drinking water for 160,000 people will be provided by the proposed Mpira-Balaka water project, which is to be part-financed by an African Development Fund loan of $11.6m. For details contact: Water Department, Ministry of Works, Private Bag 316, Capital City, Lilongwe 3. Telex 4285.

to be part-financed by a $10m credit from the International Development Association. Vehicles, equipment, civil works and various consultancy services will be required. For details contact: Ministry of Agriculture and Forestry, and Ministry of Animal Industry and Fisheries, PO Box 7003, Kampala.

Zaire

Vehicles, road and agricultural equipment, tools, fertilizers and consultancy services will be required for the Lulua Agricultural Development Project (LADP). The International Development Association has approved a loan of $21.5m. Contact:LADP, Department of Agriculture and Rural Development, BP 8722, Kinshasa.

Zambia

New government measures include an increase in import tax from 12.5 to 15%; a sales tax increase from 10 to 15%; a rise in excise duty on certain goods; a withholding tax of 30% on management fees, and a rise in the minerals tax from eight to 10%.

Zimbabwe

More than $17m is expected to be spent on railways improvement in the year from July 1985. Track improvements, and the purchase of equipment and road service vehicles are included in the plan. For details contact the National Railways of Zimbabwe, Salisbury.

● A memorandum of understanding, which could lead to future joint space projects, particularly in rocket launching and satellite technology, has been signed with the UK government.

Malaysia

Improvements to five towns, and other settlements, under the Kedah Regional Development (Sector) Project will be financed by a $45m Asian Development Bank loan. Infrastructure, housing, and public services will be improved. For details contact: Ministry of Land and Regional Development, 13th Floor, Wisma Keramat Jalan Gurney, Kuala Lumpur.

Nepal

Construction of new piped water supply systems to 75 rural communities, the installation of about 5,000 shallow tubewells with handpumps in 175 communities, and the supply of equipment, vehicles and consultancy services will be required for a rural water supplies project. The Asian Development Bank has approved a $9.6m loan to help finance the scheme.

Pakistan

Finance for the largest-ever irrigation development project for the Sind region has been approved by the World Bank

Sources of statistics

International Labour Office, *Year Book of Labour Statistics*, International Labour Office, Geneva.

Organization for Economic Cooperation and Development (OECD), *Main Economic Indicators*, OECD, Paris.

OECD, *Trade by Commodities, Series C: Vol. II Market Summaries, Exports*, OECD, Paris.

OECD, *Trade by Commodities, Series C: Vol. II Market Summaries, Imports*, OECD, Paris.

OECD, *Country Reports*, OECD, Paris.

Statistical Office of the European Communities (SOEC), *Statistical Yearbook (Eurostat)*, Office for Official Publications of the European Communities, Luxembourg.

SOEC, *Yearbook of Foreign Trade Statistics*, Office for Official Publications of the European Communities, Luxembourg.

United Nations (UN), *Demographic Yearbook*, Department of Economic and Social Affairs, Statistical Office, UN, New York.

UN, *Statistical Yearbook*, Department of Economic and Social Affairs, Statistical Office, UN, New York.

UN, *Yearbook of Industrial Statistics*, Department of Economic and Social Affairs, Statistical Office, UN, New York.

UN, *World Economic Survey* (annual), Department of Economic and Social Affairs, Statistical Office, UN, New York.

Market conditions The company's penetration of the market will be directly affected by the market conditions existing at the time of its entry. It is normally the difference or relative position of the home market vis-à-vis the export market that determines the importance of these factors.

The strengthening of the US $ against the £ sterling during 1984 allowed a speciality food manufacturer from Scotland to make considerable headway in the American market.

This category will lead to the exclusion of those countries with structural or other marketing conditions likely to increase substantially the market entry cost or lead to insuperable barriers to entry for the smaller firm. Possible criteria for the evaluation of market conditions are:

1. Strength of the currency versus sterling.
2. Import restrictions/import licences.
3. Exchange controls.
4. Level of inflation.
5. Development plans.
6. National demand preferences.
7. Salient product features, e.g. requirements for a proportion of home-produced goods.
8. Availability of sufficiently qualified intermediaries.
9. Legislative pressures.
10. Approval procedures.

Table 4
Using 'Strong currency versus sterling' criterion

149 members of the UN	Company-specific crtierion (Table 2) leaves in all countries where English is the acceptable business language.	Economic criterion (Table 3) leaves in all advanced developed countries.	*Eliminates* Australia, Canada, New Zealand, Sweden, Finland, USA. *Leaves* Benelux, Eire, Norway, Denmark, West Germany, Singapore, Japan.
	Stage 1	**Stage 2**	**Stage 3**

The array has now evolved into much more manageable proportions. This 'select' list still has a combined population five times that of the UK with vastly differing cultures and business systems.

Information sources The economic and market summaries provided by the banks are particularly valuable at this stage. A noteworthy contribution to the information stock at this level of analysis are the *Financial Times* economic surveys; a number of countries and industries are covered every year. The media can provide a mass of data. Chambers of commerce across the country run missions to a large number of markets every year. In many cases missions will have been run to the markets in question. Short market reports are normally prepared prior to the missions, and further evidence collated afterwards. Similar information can be obtained from trade associations following their missions. British exporters are very lucky in having available two excellent sources of facts concerning export prohibitions and customs procedures, in *Croner's Reference Book for Exporters*, and *Benn's Exporters' Year Book*. No serious exporter can manage without one of these. For Comecon and other state-controlled countries, the development plans are invaluable. These can normally be borrowed from the Statistics and Market Intelligence Library at 1 Victoria Street, London SW1H 0ET.

Competitive evaluation The importance of this evaluation derives from the detailed consideration of the firm's ability to win orders, often in the face of established producers, some of which will be strongly entrenched in the market. Adaptiveness to the market's particular needs and attitudes is necessary.

A small conveyor-belt manufacturer found that the way into the West German market was through a joint marketing effort with a 'rival' German manufacturer, whose range complemented the UK firm's. Now each acts as the other's agent in their home market.

Possible criteria for competitive evaluation are:

1 Product competitiveness versus established firms.
2 Company comparison with existing market structures.

3   Range and nature of existing demand.
4   Technology used in market and technical standards.
5   Structure of customer markets.
6   Nature and structure of intermediary markets.
7   Feasibility of servicing the market competitively.
8   Sales, promotional and advertising practices in the market.
9   Pricing policies, discounts, etc.
10 Levels of before- and after-sales servicing.
11 Payment terms.
12 Packaging and labelling.

Table 5
Using 'Compatible technical standards' criterion

Company-specific criterion (Table 2) leaves in all countries with English the acceptable business language.	Economic criterion (Table 3) leaves in all advanced developed economies.	Market conditions criterion (Table 4) leaves in all strong currency markets.	*Eliminates* Singapore, Japan, and Taiwan. *Leaves* Benelux, Eire, Norway, Denmark, West Germany.	These then broken down into three priority areas: 1 Benelux and West Germany. 2 Norway and Denmark. 3 Eire.
Stage 1	**Stage 2**	**Stage 3**		**Stage 4**

Information sources   For specific industries, trade associations can provide a wealth of detailed information on markets and likely competitive conditions. Often they have specific customer or intermediary information. A number of industries have the services of special export groups, e.g. the Building Materials Export Group (see Appendix 1). The services of the BOTB are very effective at this stage in market development. The network of overseas commercial attachés collates information on prices, promotional practices, likely demand and most of the identified criteria. By now the firm should be able to give the BOTB a good clear brief on its export intentions and needs. There is a wealth of published market research on overseas markets. The BOTB's *International Directory of Published Market Research* (8th edition published in 1984 in association with Arlington Management Publications Ltd) is a valuable source book; for technical standards the Technical Help for Exports Service of the British Standards Institution is an excellent service. A number of industry research associations provide technical guidance, e.g. the Furniture Industry Research Assocation.

By following this approach of eliminating markets, the company:

- Has arrived at a short list to concentrate on.
- Has built up a detailed picture of its prospective markets.
- Is aware of the compatibility between its product offering and the market's needs and capacity to use the product.
- Should be able to construct an effective sales plan and brief.
- Can identify 'fall-back' markets in full knowledge of the adaptions that will be necessary to make headway in the market.

Following this route, the depth of research is strictly related to the growth in awareness of the potential of specific markets. At the same time, more efficient use is made of the scarce resources of outside bodies. It must be emphasized that the approach is not designed to throw up surprising new markets, only the markets the firm is most likely to succeed in.

The managing director of a Nottingham-based plastic stationery company decided to concentrate further research efforts on two countries, the USA and Australia: the former because of its large population, sophisticated economy and common language; the latter because the company has recently acquired a customer there. Initial information was drawn from a number of sources, but the most significant contribution was from the BOTB library in London. None of the research, however, proved conclusive. The opportunity to visit a national trade exhibition in Chicago with a grant from the BOTB gave the company enough information to establish a very clear picture of the market in the USA.

For the more established exporter, the problem is, 'How do I differentiate from among the markets I am already servicing, and concentrate efforts?' One approach is to compare existing markets served against the criteria of (1) market attractiveness and (2) the company's standing in the market (see Figure 15).

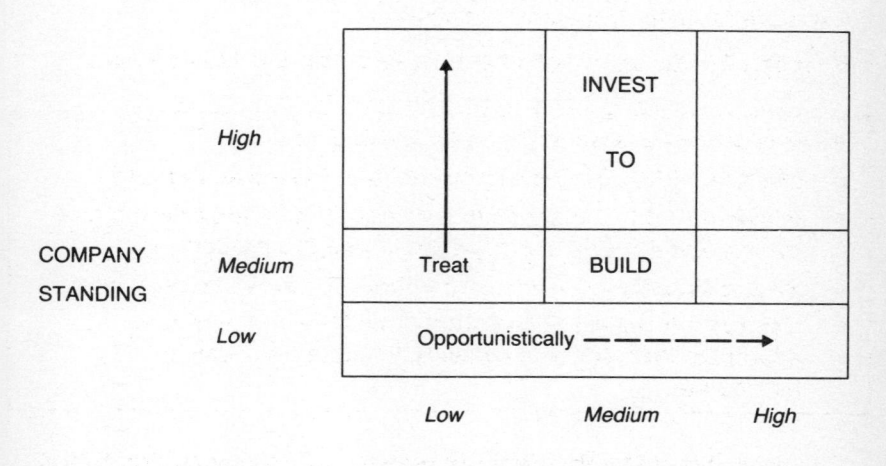

		Low	Medium	High
COMPANY STANDING	High		INVEST	
	Medium	Treat	TO BUILD	
	Low	Opportunistically ──────▶		

MARKET ATTRACTIVENESS

Figure 15

The shaded area in Figure 15 represents markets with priorities for development, while the other areas are perhaps better serviced on an opportunistic basis.

Wicksteed Leisure analysed its range of existing markets serviced against the following criteria (see Figure 16):

- Technology gap – the gap between the marketing and product technology currently being imported and that locally available.
- Ease of access – e.g. the existence of tariff barriers, import controls/licences, etc.

TECHNOLOGY GAP

		High	Low
EASE OF ACCESS	High	Saudi Arabia Oman United Arab Emirates Kuwait Bahrain	Eire Benelux West Germany Hong Kong
	Low	Algeria Yemen	

Figure 16

The firm also analysed markets against the criteria of volume sales and market growth rates (see Figure 17).

VOLUME SALES

		High	Medium	Low
MARKET GROWTH	High			Saudi Arabia
	Medium		Oman Kuwait Yemen Hong Kong	Bahrain Eire Benelux W. Germany
	Low			

Figure 17

It was decided to concentrate efforts on the Middle Eastern markets, and in particular Saudi Arabia.

Throughout this unit the terms 'country' and 'market' have been used synonymously. This is misleading, for countries are made up of many markets which in turn can be broken down into smaller market segments. Markets are not a uniform mass but customers with varying needs and requirements. Wicksteed Leisure found that customers in Saudi Arabia could be segmented by sector and users (see Figures 18 and 19).

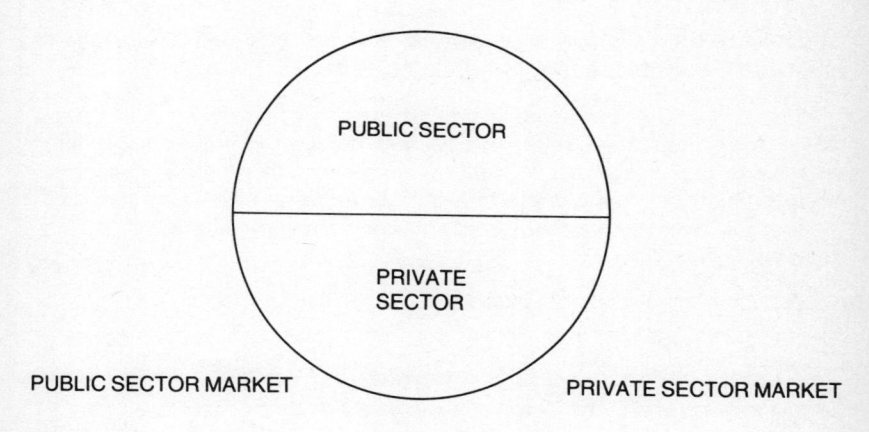

PUBLIC SECTOR

PRIVATE SECTOR

PUBLIC SECTOR MARKET   PRIVATE SECTOR MARKET

Figure 18

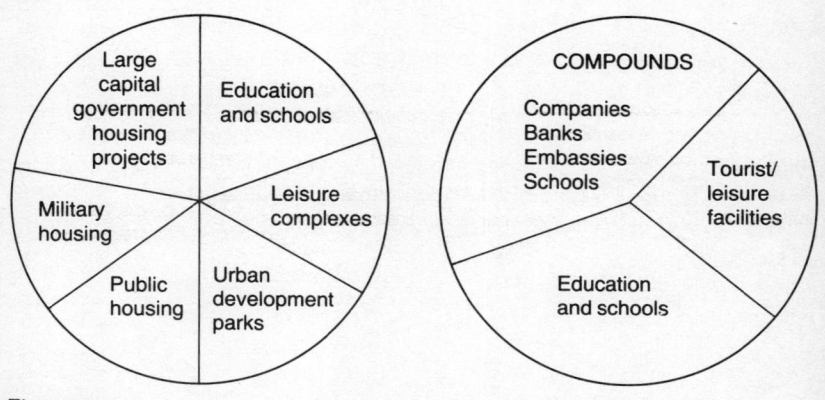

- Large capital government housing projects
- Education and schools
- Leisure complexes
- Urban development parks
- Public housing
- Military housing

COMPOUNDS
- Companies
- Banks
- Embassies
- Schools
- Tourist/leisure facilities
- Education and schools

Figure 19

109

Each of these sectors and user-segments has very different patterns of buying, service needs and design requirements. This enables Wicksteed to *get close to meeting the needs of these segments by specially tailoring products and services.* It is only worthwhile developing specialist programmes if individual segments are (1) measurable, (2) reachable, (3) substantial and (4) open to profitable commercial development.

Summary

Successful marketing in any context involves the concentration of resources against meaningful opportunities.

> 'Many British companies sell to too many markets. Most of the companies interviewed – large and small – are over-extended and are trying to do too much (in relation to the manpower and other resources available). They would be better off if they concentrated on fewer countries but more intensively.'
>
> Source: *Concentration on Key Markets*, Betro Trust (1977).

This unit aimed to reduce the bewildering array of markets and customers open to the firm to a more meaningful group worthy of more detailed research. For the established exporter, guides were provided in breaking down existing countries into more significant opportunity areas. All firms need to screen countries' (1) markets, (2) market segments, and (3) customers. The closer one gets to servicing exports customers, the more profitable exports will be.

By using this screening process, opportunities will be overlooked, but ultimate success comes from early profits in a few well-chosen markets. The purpose of the screening process is to improve the overall efficiency of the firm's personal investment in time, effort and expense.

Action Guidelines _____

1 What company-specific factors are relevant to the firm's selection of export markets?

___

2 What economic factors are relevant to the firm's selection of export markets?

___

3 What prevailing market conditions are relevant to the firm's selection of export markets?

4 What competitive factors are relevant to the firm's selection of export markets?

_____
_____
_____
_____
_____
_____
_____
_____
_____

5 What are the priority markets worthy of more detailed research or visiting?

_____
_____
_____
_____
_____
_____
_____
_____
_____

6 Locate existing markets serviced on the matrix.

	COMPANY STANDING	Low	Medium	High
High				
Medium				
Low				

MARKET ATTRACTIVENESS

8
Using the Government Support Agencies

- The complexities of exporting and market development are considerably reduced by the use of outside support agencies.
- Relationships with these agencies require careful management.
- Many of these agencies provide free services: don't underestimate their value to your business.

Introduction and aims

Although the responsibility for selling products resides internally, there is a substantial array of agencies capable and anxious to support. Most of the support is in the 'software' area, taking the form of:

1 Information.
2 Advice.
3 Counselling.
4 Training and education.

And some 'hardware' in the form of:

5 Subsidies.

Many of these services are free, nationally available and widely promoted. In reality many smaller firms have never heard of these agencies and, when contact is made, remain sceptical of the benefits and assistance they can provide. The problem when contact is made takes two forms: (1) An inability to structure inquiries in a format which these agencies can respond to; plus a corresponding failure of these organizations to adapt their patterns of response to meet small firms' needs fully. (2) Problems of mismatch, particularly in terms of time scale – 'I need the information yesterday' syndrome – and the greater or lesser specificness of the firm and its inquiries.

The aim of this unit is to:

- Highlight the range of services available.
- Identify points of access to the services (a full range of services is detailed in the appendices).
- Develop guidelines on how to build and manage relationships with the agencies.

The British Overseas Trade Board (BOTB)

Foremost among the support agencies is the BOTB, which provides financial assistance, information and advice for exporters and would-be exporters. The BOTB is also at the hub of the support agency environment; if used skilfully it can make a major contribution. To gain access to the BOTB contact should be made via one of its ten regional offices (see Appendix 2).

First impressions are important in all walks of life, and this is equally true in the opening meeting with the regional office of the BOTB. *Before contacting the BOTB regional office, do your homework.* Completion of the following check-list based on the earlier action guidelines will (1) demonstrate the level of seriousness about exports and (2) act as a useful briefing document:

Name:

Name and address of company:

Tel no.:

Size: Year established:

Description of business:

Reasons for exploring exports:

Initial export objectives:

Past export experience (including details of any representation overseas):

Key products/processes/services on offer:

Key resources:

Other agencies contacted:

Market areas of interest:

Broad area of assistance required:

Enclosures (catalogues/price lists, etc.):

A BOTB officer will be pleased to visit clients' premises and develop the brief and the role the BOTB can play in helping to meet export objectives. Don't expect the officer assigned to the case to be an expert in your particular field or to come up with immediate answers, but if used carefully he can play a key role in:

1 Introducing the firm to the full range of BOTB services.
2 Signposting other support agencies.
3 Acting as a link between the firm and the network of diplomatic and commercial services worldwide.

Building relationships If you don't feel you are getting the service you require, openly discuss your complaint. The first sign of a relationship going wrong is when one party fails to complain. The BOTB welcomes feedback and constructive criticism in the way its services are dispensed, and it is constantly looking to adapt its services to changing client needs. Leading businesspeople from the private sector with export business experience serve on the Board, and they guide and direct the government's assistance to exporters and export promotion services. Feedback facilitates this process.

Once relations have been established, the second lesson in building the relationship is *communication*. As far as it is possible, keep the regional office regularly informed of progress or lack of progress. There is nothing more dispiriting for the regional office than to activate a number of avenues of investigation, gather information from the post, put the client into contact with other agencies and then hear nothing. A quarterly telephone call to update the regional office will suffice. This will keep the file pending, and the firm's specific export requirements will continue to receive attention.

What can the BOTB do for me?

The services offered by the BOTB cover three broad areas:

- The collection and dissemination of market intelligence.
- Trade promotion.
- Individual schemes for UK exporters.

The collection and dissemination of market intelligence This provides insights into specific market opportunities, such as through the Export Intelligence Service (EIS), and the extremely useful 'Hints to Exporters' series and 'Country Profiles'. In the screening process of world markets, a clear picture of the tariffs, import and trade regulations is necessary. The eight market branches provide an invaluable and up-to-date service to exporters. The level of foreign duties or import quotas is crucial when calculating the profitability of servicing a particular market.

The Board has sixteen 'area advisory groups' responsible, on a geographical basis, for providing advice on the world's main trading areas. The Worlds Aid Section collects and monitors information on world aid programmes and disseminates this through the EIS.

Contact point
World Aid Section, 1 Victoria Street, London SW1H 0ET
(01-215 3997/8).

Information note The following documents explaining how the various aid agencies work are available free of charge:

- World Bank: *Guidelines for Procurement*; *Uses of Consultants*; *Withdrawal of Loans and Credits*.

- Asian Development Bank (ADB): *Questions and Answers*; *Guidelines for Procurement*; *Uses of Consultants*; *ADB Basic Information*.
- Inter-American Development Bank (IDB): *Use of Counselling Firms*; *Basic Facts about the Inter-American Development Bank*.

A vast amount of published information on overseas markets is available at the Statistics and Market Intelligence Library (SMILS), and the Product Data Store.

Contact point
SMILS and Product Data Store, 1 Victoria Street, London, SW1H 0ET. Open Monday to Friday, 9.30 a.m. to 5.30 p.m.

Often the picture of markets gained through these services, backed by the approaches identified earlier on selecting markets (Unit 7), will stimulate firms to visit the market to win orders or carry out in-market research.

Export Marketing Research Scheme An ideal vehicle to visit and research export markets is the Export Marketing Research Scheme, operated by the BOTB. Marketing research has been defined as *the systematic gathering, recording, analysis and interpretation of data on problems relating to the market for, and the marketing of, goods and services*. This may sound full of jargon, but in reality marketing research will help you attain (1) better informed decision-making about exports and (2) a lower level of risks involved in exports. Marketing research is an essential part of winning export sales. The BOTB scheme provides both a free professional overseas marketing research advisory service, and financial support for export marketing research.

The director of a small company manufacturing safety products for the chemical, petrochemical and transport industries wanted to research the potential of his newly developed products within the USA market. The research objectives were:

- To establish sales prospects for the products and determine whether it was worthwhile for the company to enter the market.
- To determine current or pending government health and safety regulations.
- To determine whether existing distribution methods and channels were suited to handling the product.
- To determine whether the product was technically acceptable in terms of US product liability insurance and whether it offered any advantages to users.
- To determine the extent and performance of alternative safety systems in comparison to the firm's own product.

An itinerary of interviews with: users, distributors, health and safety bodies and British counsuls was scheduled for the period 20 March to 7 April 1984.

A formal proposal with costings was put to the BOTB. The Board agreed that the director was experienced enough to carry out research 'of a standard equal to that of a professional marketing research consultant or agency', and financial support of 50% of essential travel costs and daily allowance was provided on receipt of the research report. (This remains confidential to the firm carrying out the research.) This reduced the costs of the research trip from £2500 to £1250.

The Export Marketing Research Scheme is of real practical relevance and support to the small firm exporter.

Contact:
BOTB, Export Marketing Research Section, 1 Victoria Street, London SW1H 0ET (01-215 5277 (firms A–E) 01-215 3173 (firms F–M) 01-215 5272 (firms N–Z)).

Information note The BOTB is joint publisher of the *International Directory of Market Research Organizations*, *The International Directory of Published Market Research*, and a free booklet, *Industrial Marketing Researchers' Check-list*.

The Export Marketing Research Section commissions research whose results are made available. During 1983 a study was carried out to assess the market for personal sports equipment, clothing and footwear in nineteen Middle East countries, in order to assist individual UK companies to improve their export performance in these countries.

Trade promotions This is the largest area of BOTB expenditure and support in the critical area of bringing seller face to face with buyer. Presenting British industry abroad through trade fairs assists both the firms participating and the overall image of British industry. The major areas of activity are:

1 Overseas exhibitions.
2 Retail promotions.
3 Outward missions.
4 Seminars and symposia.

Considerable practical and financial help is available to the first-time exporter, with a sliding scale of support for more experienced firms.

Contact point

BOTB, Fairs and Promotions Branch, Dean Bradley House, 52 Horseferry Road, London SW1P 2AG (01-212 7276).

Information note   A full programme of support for British industry at overseas trade fairs is published at quarterly intervals in the official journal of the Department of Trade and Industry, *British Business*.

The search for sales by UK firms is matched by the search for purchases and information by possible customers. Their buying and information-gathering visits to the UK gain considerable support from the BOTB.

Contact point

BOTB, Inward Missions Section, Dean Bradley House, 52 Horseferry Road, London SW1P 2AG (01-212 8758)

Individual schemes for UK exporters The Market Prospects Service gives information about the prospects of selling goods and services overseas, and advice on how best to go about it.

Contact point
Regional BOTB office.

The Export Representative Service helps the exporter locate the best form of local representation whether it be an agent, distributor or importer. They can also help in finding a partner to manufacture under licence. Negotiations are, of course, entirely between the firm and selected representatives.

Contact point
Regional BOTB office.

These services cost £150 and £100 respectively, but if the report is followed up by a visit to the market, the fees will be refunded as a contribution towards travel costs. A word of warning: these reports take up to eight weeks to compile.

The Overseas Status Report Services give an independent commercial assessment of potential overseas representatives as well as useful advice on the complex and changing area of overseas agency legislation.

Contact point
Regional BOTB office.

The Market Entry Guarantee Scheme (MEGS) has recently been set up to assist smaller firms to break into new export markets by providing half-funding for new initiatives and sharing the risks involved. Initiatives may include the establishment of an overseas sales office and the recruitment of local staff to service the market. Funds are repayable with interest through a levy on sales to the market. The minimum funding for any one venture is £15 000, the maximum £300 000.

> **Contact point**
> MEGS, Unit 1, 1 Victoria Street, London SW1H 0ET (01-215 5751).

The Projects and Export Policy Division (PEP) administers overseas project funds to offset some of the pre-contractual expenses of pursuing major capital projects overseas. It is unlikely to be of relevance to the smaller firm unless operating within a consortium of firms.

Other government services

Government services to exporters go far beyond the work of the BOTB. The Ministry of Defence, for example, runs a Defence Sales Organization (DSO) to help firms market and sell their defence products and services overseas.

> **Contact point**
> Director of Marketing Services, DSO, Room 707, Stuart House, 23–25 Soho Square, London W1V 5FG (01-632 4826)

Other ministries, such as the DHSS, are becoming increasingly export orientated. Any firm servicing the needs of a particular government department, e.g. supplying the National Health Service, should contact the Ministry in its initial search for export business.

The Central Office of Information (COI) Publicity and promotion are recognized by the government as a part of successful marketing. The COI is the centre of the government's world-wide publicity network. It can be, and frequently is, geared to the promotional needs of the UK exporter. The COI will be interested in a *newsworthy* story.

> Oilab Lubrication Ltd of Wolverhampton designed and developed a DIY portable oil and lubricant analysis unit under the trade mark OILAB. The unit is smartly packed into a rigid aluminium briefcase,

and allows 'in-house' lubricant and fuel analysis with the minimum of disruption or down-time. It is particularly useful for operatives on ships and oil rigs. The story of the development of this unit by a one-man business was distributed world-wide by the COI. Oilab Lubrication Ltd received over 100 inquiries, and as a result of the press story is now actively pursuing the sales and distribution of the unit in the Mexico Gulf area around Houston. An export market research award from the BOTB helped Oilab visit and carry out interviews within the area.

Contact point
See Appendix 3.

HM Customs and Excise This is the point of departure for goods and critical to the process of exporting and importing. They play a very positive role in Britain's overseas trade – guiding, advising and helping firms. A complex array of tax reliefs, duty exemptions and payments surrounds overseas trade. The local Customs and Excise office will assist the exporter to avoid problems and satisfy the necessary export regulations and formalities. Customs and Excise are required by law to apply documentation procedures, and although they will help when possible, carefully completed documentation is essential.

The Simplification of International Trade Procedure (SITPRO) This is the key government organization working on simplified systems of documentation. The main features of its work are described in the unit on documentation (Unit 14).

Contact point

SITPRO, Almack House, 26–28 King Street, London SW1Y 6QW (01-214 3399).

Information note Although a knowledge of export documentation is necessary, many small firms find that employing a reputable freight forwarder is an inexpensive method of minimizing documentation problems. Such forwarders will advise on the packing and marking of consignments and customs requirements;

make out the various transport documents; arrange the best shipment route and even transport the goods themselves. This service is usually between 3% and 5% of total freight costs.

Contact point

Institute of Freight Forwarders, Suffield House, 9 Paradise Road, Richmond, Surrey TW9 1SA (01-948 3141).

But remember to shop around and obtain a number of quotes.

Exports Credits Guarantee Department (ECGD) This government department assists exporters in two main ways: (1) by insuring exporters against the risks of not being paid by their overseas customers; (2) by giving guarantees to banks under which companies may obtain finance for their export credit transactions. Note that the ECGD provides cover, not funds. The specific details of ECGD services, and their interplay with the overall financing of exports, are covered in the unit on finance (Unit 13).

National Economic Development Office (NEDO) NEDO produces and disseminates some very useful reports. For example, in 1981 it produced *Spearhead Finance: Increasing the Exports of UK Knitwear to France*. These are usually compiled by 'sector working parties', which are industry-specific.

Contact point

NEDO, Millbank Tower, Millbank, London SW1P 4QX (01-211 3000).

Scottish Development Agency (SDA) Scottish exporting firms should contact the SDA Small Business Division, Trade Promotions Manager.

Contact point:

SDA, Roseberry House, Haymarket Terrace, Edinburgh EH12 5EZ (031-337 9595).

Scottish Council (Development and Industry) Sponsors outward missions, organizes seminars and gives assistance in marketing and selling abroad.

Contact point
Scottish Council (Development and Industry), 23 Chester Street, Edinburgh EH3 7ET (031-225 7911).

Summary

Recent research* has revealed that many smaller firms are not aware of the BOTB and fail to make effective use of its services. Some users criticize the system for being unwieldy and unresponsive; they claim, for example, that it takes far too long to receive payment for travel and expenses to overseas exhibitions – a time lag which many smaller firms cannot afford. However, these difficulties do not undermine the fact that the BOTB spends over £50m on export promotion per annum, is at the heart of government efforts to encourage and develop UK exports and, if used correctly, is capable of providing a full range of support services for the smaller firm. The procedure recommended is:

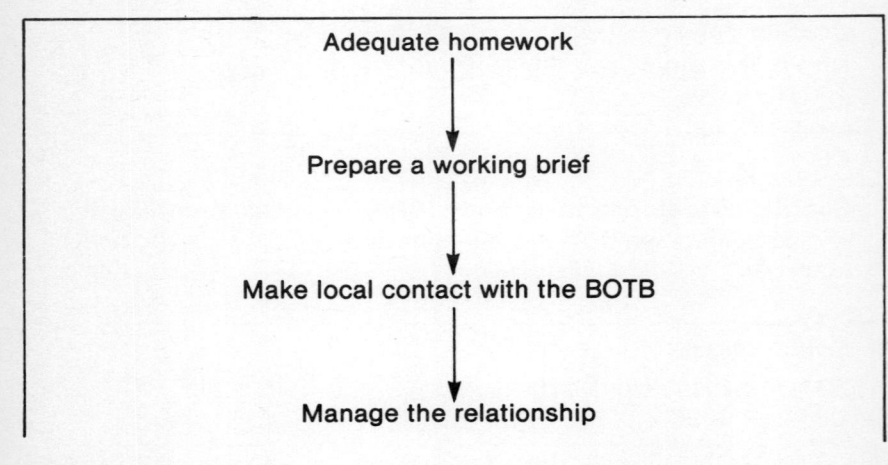

Adequate homework
↓
Prepare a working brief
↓
Make local contact with the BOTB
↓
Manage the relationship

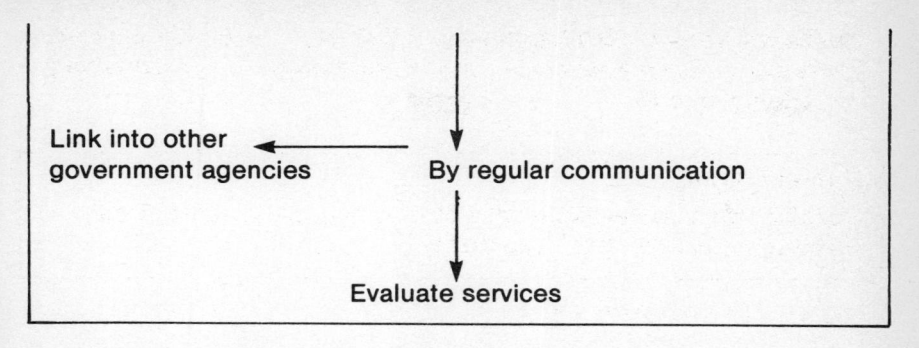

```
              ↓
Link into other  ←———
government agencies        By regular communication
                              ↓
                        Evaluate services
```

Allow adequate time to manage the relationship.

* R. George and G. Burg, *Help for Small Firms*, a review of BOTB services in relation to small firms, 1984 prepared by the BOTB.

Action Guidelines _____

Evaluation of government support services

	Date contacted	Contact	Useful	Of little use
Export Intelligence Service				
'Hints to Exporters' series				
World Aid Section				
Statistics and Market Intelligence Library				
Product Data Store				
Exports Marketing Research Section				
International directories				
Trade promotions				
British Business				
Inward Missions Section				
Market Prospects Service				
Export Representative Service				
Overseas Status Report Service				
Market Entry Guarantee Scheme				
Projects and Export Policy Division				
Other government services				
Central Office of Information				
HM Customs and Excise				
Simplification of International Trade Procedure				
Export Credits Guarantee Department				
National Economic Development Office				
Scottish Development Agency				
Scottish Council				

9
Using the Commercial Support Services

- Because they cost money, commercial services require even more careful briefing and management.
- Some services provide market- and industry-specific information and advice.
- Commercial services provide facilities and assistance on most export problems.

Introduction and aims

Outside of the government services there exists a growing commercial network of suppliers eager to service the needs of the small firm sector. They are able to provide help as diverse as telex facilities, translation services, consultancy help and training – mostly at a cost. This unit introduces the major suppliers, how to access them and make the most of their services.

Bank services to exporters

The London clearing banks Their guidance on finance, payment, credit, currencies and sometimes pricing remains at the hub of the clearing banks' services to exports. Radiating from this has developed a wide selection of other forms of help: business references, market information, economic intelligence, documentation services, overseas contacts through world-wide banking links, and insights derived from working with many exporters. The more general facets of export finance are dealt with later (Unit 13), but other aspects of bank services are worth noting here.

All exports involve expenses and some delays before full payment arrives. The bank should be involved in this process to help with the normal short- to medium-term overdrafts; it can also help with finance through its specialist companies and divisions, e.g. Barclays Mercantile Factoring.

The world-wide network of information and activity of the banks means that they can advise on the possible difficulties, e.g. exchange control problems, that may develop with certain customer countries. In all circumstances, it is important to know about current trading regulations concerning the nations the firm is dealing with. The bank should be in a position to guide the company on this.

Invoicing raises a number of important issues which the bank should be able to assist with. Methods of payment, particularly non-sterling payment, have caused problems for some firms. The banks are experts in handling money, and their acquired knowledge should be employed in the thorny area of currency handling. There are, broadly speaking, four payment systems: (1) *open account*, (2) *goods on consignment*, (3) *bills for collection* and (4) *letters of credit*. Before adopting a particular system, or using a specific method, discuss it at length with your bank manager. He knows you, he knows your company, he will point you in the right direction.

Britain is still the banking centre of the world. In consequence, Britain's banks have extensive overseas links. There is a constant gathering of information. All banks offer a credit information service. On occasion, they are approached by prospective buyers, agents or distributors and they pass these contacts back to their customers. The firm intending to make an overseas visit (particularly the first visit) is strongly advised to make contact with the office in the country through its local bank branch.

Ultimately the only export successes are those that secure payment. Insurance is an essential part of this process. The banks are able to give considerable guidance and advice on the necessity of cover and the most appropriate form.

All the major clearing banks have an overseas or international division. Very often, the information and advice gleaned for the firm derives from this source. Making contact with the international division at an early date is a useful step. In the decision to export, and in the export process itself, the company's bank should be actively involved and its powerful aid enlisted.

The merchant banks These perform a more limited service to prospective exporters. They are particularly involved in the funding of projects under ECGD cover termed *buyer credit*. These involve contracts of £1m or more where buyers need to find their 'front end' and 'back end' finance from other sources. In developing this type of project there are complex arrangements to be made and the bank actively participates in this process from an early stage. Their major roles lie in building up the loan, establishing competitive interest rates and agreeing the premium. At the same time, many of the merchant banks have developed their own political and financial information base, often with country specialists, enabling them to build up a full picture of forward risk, economic climates, and the risks involved in dealings with specific countries.

International and foreign banks A research study in 1977 noted that 22% of firms in overseas trade had used an American bank in the UK and 23% another foreign bank. (Many firms use more than one bank.) Although many of their services reflect those of the UK banks, international and foreign banks may have:

- Access to sources of credit not available to UK banks.
- Greater flexibility on charging and interest.
- Strength in particular areas, e.g. Algemene Bank Netherland in South America.

Banking services are purchased and ought to be evaluated in the same manner as any bought-in service.

Trade associations

There are a number of associations which:

> - Provide advice and guidance on particular aspects of exports.
> - Supply detailed market information relevant to firms in their industry.
> - Organize outward and inward trade missions and exhibitions.
> - Represent the interests of exporting firms in their industry to UK and overseas governments.

Many services designed to meet the needs of their members have been developed. These may involve:

1 Market information.
2 Trade opportunities.
3 Tariff, finance and documentation services.
4 Promotional activity.
5 Organizing exhibitions and fairs.
6 Missions.

Market information Many trade associations have accumulated a substantial data bank on export opportunities in particular countries for their membership. Although these are sometimes brought together in special reports, particularly when a trade mission is planned, the bulk is usually available in an unstructured form on request. The great strength of their information is that it is specific to a particular industry and frequently assembled from the reports of practicising exporters.

> The marketing manager of an East Midlands machine tool company contacted for the first time the Machine Tools Trade Association, for information on the American market.
>
> 'I was pleasantly surprised at the information they could provide. They have their own marketing executive who knows by name the various contact points at the BOTB and the consuls in North America. He produced reports on visits to markets by members of the association; he came up with some

> staggering figures on the percentage of machine tool sales and, more important for my business, what percentage of these were vertical machining tools. He recommended the *American Machinist Journal*, which is full of information.'

Trade opportunities The last few years have witnessed a growing feeling of mutual help among UK exporters. British firms are much more ready to feed back specific opportunities they hear of but which are outside of their sphere. Often they are reported to the trade association, which will inform companies in the particular area of operation. Foreign buyers sometimes approach trade associations directly for contacts and suppliers.

Tariff, finance and documentation services The overwhelming majority of trade associations actively involve themselves in attempts to influence government policy-making. This keeps them in the forefront of information on tariffs, finance and documentation. Their discussions with government officials enable them to keep abreast of overseas developments. This is coordinated with the dissemination of information on these developments to prospective and existing exporters.

> *Information note* Many trade associations have built up substantial libraries. They represent an invaluable data base, the extent of which should be explored and used regularly.

Promotional activity In exports, this takes two forms in most trade associations: (1) promoting the interests of the industry and (2) promoting specific events, e.g. export success seminars, to member firms.

Organizing exhibitions and fairs The critical role of these in exports has long been recognized by trade associations. They involve themselves in a number of direct ways:

1 Sponsoring UK exhibitions and promoting them overseas.
2 Assisting member firms to exhibit overseas.

3   Attending key international exhibitions to represent the industry and glean information.
4   Organizing joint venture stands, i.e. where a number of firms exhibit together.

An up-to-date picture of the trade association's exhibition activity should be kept by member firms.

Trade missions   Trade associations are the principal sponsoring organizations for *vertical outward trade missions*, i.e. where the members are drawn primarily from a specific industry. These have the great advantage of providing scope for in-depth study by the mission organizations, concentration of effort by resident commercial attachés and a direct cross-fertilization of information. The association will normally handle all travel and accommodation arrangements, providing access to group rates; besides being a recognized sponsoring organization, this provides access to BOTB missions grants.

The last few years have seen a growing recognition of the value of *inward trade missions*. These enable a group of foreign businesspeople to visit plants and factories in the UK at a heavily subsidized rate.

Trade association services, as outlined in this brief overview, vary considerably by industry, and their special facilities should be identified. Costs are usually very reasonable.

Information note   For details and addresses of trade associations, particularly if the services of more than one trade association may be relevant, refer to the *Directory of British Associations*, CBD Publications.

The CBI

The Confederation of British Industry, as the representative of UK industry, receives many trade inquiries from overseas. It can therefore assist smaller member firms to make contact with export markets. The CBI has a network of regional offices.

Chambers of commerce and industry

The services of these bodies cover most facets of exporting, ranging from documentation through to the organization of overseas missions. A number of chambers are authorized to issue ATA ('admission temporaire – temporary admission') carnets, and some supply certificates of origin. You can use an international customs document, called an *ATA carnet*, to cover the temporary export of certain goods (commercial samples, exhibits for international trade fairs abroad and professional equipment) to countries which are parties to the ATA Convention in respect of those goods, and cover the re-import of such goods into the UK.

All exporters should familiarize themselves with the export services of the local chamber. This will probably lead to some degree of involvement and access to its facilities. It is worth recognizing that, although the formal services are very useful, the informal contacts are frequently the most valuable.

- *Agents.* Assistance in location and appointment.
- *Buyers.* Lists and visits.
- *Capacity register.* Available for reference.
- *Education.* Programmes.
- *Export documentation.* Can be supplied and advice given.
- *Export marketing.* Missions.
- *Import regulations.* Information.
- *Information.* Data bank.
- *Legal.* Advice and services.
- *Library.* Open to members.
- *Standards and codes of practice.* Available.
- *Telex.* Group service.
- *Translations and interpretation.* Available.

Source: extracted from *Guide to Birmingham Chamber of Commerce and Industry*.

A small foundry built up its initial presence in the USA from a contact made through the local chamber of commerce.

The essential feature in this example was the willingness of the firm to follow up actively the insights and contacts made in the informal environment. The message of '*perception – persistence – practice*' is clearly illustrated:

- *Perception.* An opportunity is seen and recognized.
- *Persistence.* The firm follows it up, managing to cope with set-backs.
- *Practice.* The company tackles the customer, meets his or her requirements and is paid.

One of the strengths of the chambers of commerce is their access to national and international bodies: the Association of British Chambers of Commerce, and the International Chamber of Commerce. Both bodies draft guidelines for action. In some cases, their statements are definitive: e.g. *Incoterms 1953*, issued by the International Chamber of Commerce, defining policies and conditions governing packing, insurance and delivery (see Unit 14 on documentation).

A number of international links have been built through chambers of commerce, e.g. the Anglo-German Chamber of Commerce; the Netherlands–British Chamber of Commerce. These are committed to building links of understanding and trade between their respective countries (see Appendix 4), and their membership is made up primarily of businesspeople specializing in both countries. They frequently have access to information, and their contacts can make access to the relevant markets much less difficult.

Industry research associations

British industry is well served with research associations whose primary objectives are often to improve the techniques and practices of firms in their industries. Although their activities are normally directed towards products and production, their role in the export process should not be neglected. Common criticisms of

UK production – poor adaptation to market conditions; insufficient quality control; inadequate packing – fall firmly in the areas of responsibility of the various industry trade associations.

The overwhelming majority offer facilities to test materials for different climatic and other conditions, providing guidelines on areas of adaptation and development, e.g. to meet tropical conditions. Advice can be obtained from the Packaging Division of the Research Association for the Paper and Board, Printing and Packaging Industries (PIRA) in the critical area of export packaging. A number of research associations will even give guidance of technical requirements to firms outside their immediate industry. They may also provide library services and specialized consultancy.

The British Standards Institution

No discussion of technical specifications can ignore the role of the British Standards Institution (BSI) with its specialized Technical Help for Exporters. The BSI is an independent body, authorized to prepare national standards in the UK and cooperate with similar bodies in drawing up international or common standards. In this role, it is part of the daily life of most firms. However, the plethora of standards and regulations across the world has led to the BSI adopting an active part in assisting British firms to meet these standards.

These services extend across the whole gamut of advice on problems affecting technical specifications on products and processes, right through to supplying details on overseas national and provincial regulations. Although these services are extremely useful, the fees charged are high. There is a free trial offer of £100 worth of financial advice for small firms, which helps offset these fees.

Contact point
Technical Help for Exporters, BSI, Linford Wood, Milton Keynes MK14 6LE (0908 320033).

Other agencies

Export clubs There are informal organizations founded on a regional basis and usually linked with a local chamber of commerce and industry. The major benefit they offer the small exporter is the opportunity to access the knowledge of experienced exporters and obtain up-to-date information.

Development and enterprise agencies These are of growing importance in the work to build up the industrial strength of their region. Many of them encourage and foster export development.

Local authorities Many local authorities are actively engaged in the promotion of their areas in overseas markets. This takes the form of 'twinning', 'exchanges' and organizing small exhibitions of locally produced goods and services overseas.

Commercial concerns Representing a wide selection of interests geared to help exporters for a return, they cover the areas of:

1   Marketing research.
2   Consultancy.
3   Training.
4   Shipping and documentation.

Institutes The Institute of Export and the Institute of Marketing are active in offering education and training support. Both operate a strong regional network.

Contact point

Institute of Export, 64 Clifton Street, London EC2A 411B (01-247 9812).

Institute of Marketing, Moor Hall, Cookham, Berks SL6 9QH (06285 24922).

Summary

Despite the wide range of services mentioned here there are still some groups we have not covered. We do not recommend contacting them all, but many of these services have played and continue to play an important role in the country's exporting performance. At the centre of this service network is the BOTB, and the regional office should be at the top of your shopping list. Before you approach them, *be adequately prepared*, and aim to utilize them *efficiently*. Many firms 'write off' the BOTB following their first meeting.

> 'They just loaded us with leaflets but did not seem to be prepared to offer real practical assistance' – *(managing director of a small engineering firm.)*

This is a mistake. The BOTB is an important source of advice and help as well as providing 'hardware' support in the form of the MEGS and EMR scheme. Relationships with the BOTB require careful management and development. As the firm moves forward in exports, contacts will develop with commercial agencies; firms will not want to join or use them all, but should select them at the relevant stages of the firm's export development (see the action guidelines). Remember that these agencies are there to support export efforts – they will not do all the work for the firm.

Action Guidelines

Developing the business	Servicing sales	Making sales	Establishing representation	Overseas visit	More detailed research and promotion	Risk research and market screening	Evaluating report growth option	Agencies/services
	*		*	*	*			Regional BOTB office
							*	Small firms counselling service
					*			World Aid Section
	*	*	*					World Aid Section
*								Area Advisory Group
*		*						EIS
*				*	*			SMILS
*		*	*	*				EMRS
*		*	*	*				Fairs and promotions
*		*						Inward missions
*				*				Market prospects
*								MEGS
*			*					Overseas status reports
*		*						Government ministries
*				*				COI
	*				*			Customs and Excise
	*							SITPRO
	*							EGCD
	*				*		*	Banks
		*	*	*	*			Trade associations
		*						CBI
*	*		*	*		*		Chamber of commerce
*			*	*				Chamber of commerce
*				*	*			Ind. Research Assoc.
				*	*			THE
*							*	Export chambers
					*		*	Development agencies
								Institutes
		*			*			Local authorities
							*	Accountant

10
Managing Market Research

- Data and information are an external resource.
- The collection of data and information needs to be managed on an on-going basis.
- Marketing research provides the corner-stone in attempts to manage the future.

Introduction and aims

The considerable amount of data and information that flows from marketing research enables managers to:

- Identify product/market opportunities.
- Make more informed decisions about the way they manage, plan and control their marketing operations.
- Keep in touch with what is happening in the changing market-place.

In reality, smaller concerns doubt the impact marketing research can make on their business and prefer to rely on experience and 'intuitive' feel for the market. The complexity of winning and retaining business overseas, and the amount of information available, require a more rigorous and professional attitude to marketing research. It needs to be approached in a *systematic* way, and viewed as a *two-way flow* between the firm and its markets/customers – with the *realization* that, although uncertainty and risk will be reduced, marketing research does not provide all of the anwers.

Despite talk of the 'information revolution', its collection and analysis remain a complex and often time-consuming task. This chapter seeks to (1) alert you to the variety of sources of information and (2) suggest low-cost ways of carrying out market research.

The terms 'data', 'information' and 'intelligence' are often used synonymously and require some clarification. Data comprises statistical facts presented in some specific format; information is descriptive and adds flesh to the bones of raw data; whilst the gathering, recording, analysis and interpretation of data and information provides a firm with the intelligence it can act on. Most marketing research begins with the definition of a marketing problem or the setting of research objectives: in the previous sections we saw how marketing research helped reduce worldwide marketing opportunities into a number of priority markets worthy of more detailed research. Therefore research objectives should be:

1 Commercially worthwhile.
2 Specific.
3 Achievable.

Information and data sources

A useful way of dividing sources of information and data is in terms of location and type (see Figure 20). In the search for data and information, managers are advised to check out each of these sources in the suggested sequence 1, 2, 3, 4. This will ensure that the more difficult and costly sources will be tackled only after easier, cheaper avenues have been tried.

LOCATION

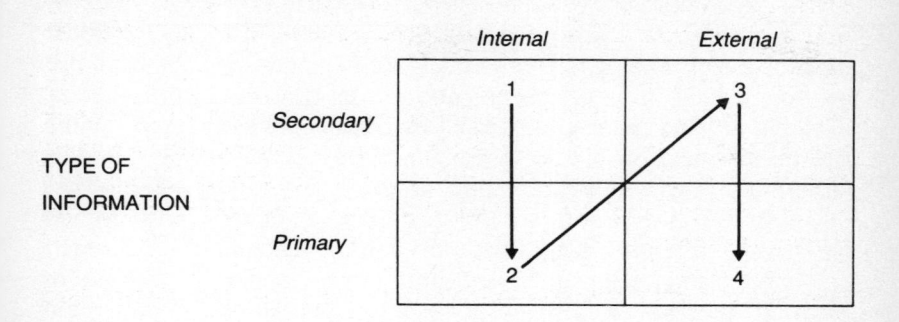

	Internal	External
Secondary	1 ↓	3 ↗
Primary	2	4 ↓

TYPE OF INFORMATION

Figure 20

Internal secondary information This category corresponds to the information outlined in the unit on past export experience (Unit 3), i.e. the information which exists within the firm and which may be put to a more productive use. This includes:

- Overseas trip reports.
- Delivery records.
- Complaints/returns.
- Tender records.
- Sales analysis.
- Contact records.
- Customer records.
- Order book.
- Competitors' catalogues.
- Competitors' price lists.
- Competitors' products.
- Competitors' advertising material.

A packaging company analysed entries in the UK exhibition visitors' book and exhibition handbook to locate potential manufacturers and distributors in overseas markets.

Internal primary information This involves gathering information which may not exist in a written form or within company reports. It can involve questioning existing staff or gathering new information from existing systems.

External secondary information Generally the search for additional insight into the market-place will mean going outside the company for data. External secondary information exists outside the firm, and has previously been collected and reported by some individual or organization, e.g. government statistics, newspaper and journal articles, market research reports. This information may be stored in conventional forms – reports, books, directories, etc. – but increasing amounts are being handled by new technologies such as Prestel, Ceefax, Oracle and on-line data-bases. It is the computerization and abstracting of data which has made access or desk research much easier. Providers of external sources of information can be divided into three main categories:

1 Government.
2 Commercial.
3 Educational.

Government sources are often free and easily accessible. Commercial services can be expensive but reduce the amount of time spent in carrying out desk research. Educational establishments are an important, but often overlooked, source of information: they carry out their own research and act as a channel for wider sources of information. Don't be intimidated by the prospect of approaching the local university or polytechnic; as a taxpayer the firm is a stake-holder in their activities. Many of them are encouraging closer links with industry and developing collaborative schemes such as science and innovation parks where there is a free flow of research ideas and new developments.

It is not the intention of this book to detail all the sources of secondary information available to the exporter. That would be impossible in a volume of this size. Within the action guidelines, we list some of the major questions managers raise about secondary sources and provide some of the answers. You will need help in locating and using secondary sources, and apart from the BOTB information service, your local library will assist. Libraries have shown spectacular changes in their ability to provide commercial information. Many now have a 'commercial intelligence officer' and are computer linked to national and international networks. 'Network', for instance, is an information service linking libraries in the North-east of England. It offers a specialist inquiry service and technical, commercial and scientific information. By stepping into a town library, Network provides access to:

1. Foreign trade, commercial and telephone directories.
2. Overseas trade statistics.
3. Current economic data on overseas countries.
4. Complete sets of EEC documents.
5. Depository collections of British, European, PCT and American patent specifications.
6. Complete sets of British Standards, and large collections of standards and specifications issued by other bodies, e.g. ACI, ANSS, API, ASTM, DEF, DIN, OCMA, SAE.
7. Air, bus, rail and shipping timetables.

Some local libraries are linked to international data-bases such as Lockheed. Searches take time and cost money, and it is important the firm knows the purpose of the research and can communicate this to the member of the library staff handling the inquiry. A telephone call in advance will enable staff to make the necessary searches and have items located and ready. Firms operating in new and developing fields face particular information problems. It is frustrating to find that the firm's product classification does not fit or is aggregated with other product groupings within the Standard Industrial Classification (SIC). Trade statistics are notoriously difficult to follow, and commercial information can often be out of date.

A manufacturer of specialist fitness equipment was researching export potential within the Middle East. Consulting UK export figures for 1982, it discovered that its product category was 'lumped in' under the heading of 'Gymnasium equipment' (SIC 97.06.1010), offering no real clues of export potential.

These are real problems. It takes time to build a picture of a market operating at arms' length; and it requires skills of detection and objectivity.

Doing your own research

External primary information Not all of the information required to make decisions about exports is available from secondary sources. Primary or original research involves information gathering from informants outside of the firm, such as interviewing buyers to establish buying motives and how existing products satisfy their needs. This type of research requires:

1 Specialist research skills.
2 Knowledge of research methods.
3 Money.
4 Time in the field.

If these research skills exist within the firm, the Export Marketing Research Scheme of the BOTB can reduce primary research costs and provide assistance on methods of information gathering. An external market research agency or consultant can be expensive, although the scheme will grant aid up to 50% of the total costs. (This does not cover research undertaken within the countries of the EEC.) Other ways of reducing costs are:

- Multi-client studies: where a group of non-competing manufacturers with a common interest in a specific market commission research. (The EMR scheme grants aid for the purchase of multi-client studies up to 33⅓% of the total cost.)
- Omnibus surveys: a survey undertaken at regular intervals on behalf of several clients, each of whom commissions a number of the questions.
- Telephone interviewing.

Direct dialling and reduced charges enable researchers to carry out a speedy and cheap telephone survey of respondents across a wide geographical area. The telephone gives immediate access to the offices of buyers, intermediaries and government agencies.

Using external consultants

All research involves a trade-off with time – the most valuable resource. Subcontracting the research to another party will save time but remove you from the important process of building up a clear picture of customers and markets and learning about competitive influences. It is, after all, you who will be negotiating and winning the business; it is you who know most about the business, and it may be unwise to distance yourself too much from the 'coal face'. Early 'hands-on' experience in gathering export information develops confidence, reveals the wealth of information available and aids decision-making. Any decision to use an external agency or consultant should be conditional on:

1 A summary of information gathered from categories 1, 2 and 3.
2 A brief on what you want the consultancy/agency to do, and where their experience should lie.
3 A budget.

Information source   For a list of consultants/agencies, contact:
Market Research Society, 15 Belgrave Square, London SW1X 8PF (01-235 4709).

The Society provides a directory entitled *Organizations Providing Marketing Research Services in Great Britain*.

A useful method of getting primary research carried out on a reasonable budget is the Scanmark project. This is run by post-graduate students, who carry out field assignments on an 'expenses only' basis.

Contact point
Scanmark, Bucks College of Higher Education, High Wycombe, Bucks HP11 2JZ (0494 22141).

Always take up references and talk through the research brief with a number of agencies/consultants. Ask for a proposal with full details on costings and timings. Beware of 'cowboys'.

Summary

Marketing research provides the basis for decisions about marketing:

- Which products/services should I sell?
- Which products/services require adaptation for overseas markets?
- How should I promote my products/services?
- How should I price my products/services?
- What after-sales service should I offer?
- How should I make my products/services available to the market?

This is not an aimless gathering of information which is 'nice to know', but a directed, managed and coordinated effort to gather information which meets company objectives. Information sources can be divided into:

1 Internal secondary.
2 Internal primary.
3 External secondary.
4 External primary.

Internal sources are easily overlooked but can provide a rich source of information. The revolution in information technology has made external secondary sources of information more accessible to the smaller firm. Local libraries play an important part in helping to access this data: the relationship with the local library or commercial intelligence officer requires managing:

1 Provide them with a brief.
2 Allow them enough time.
3 Keep them informed of progress.

Export sales, like new domestic sales, cannot be initiated on the cheap. Part of the firm's investment will take the form of field research to establish market/sales potential. This may be undertaken either by in-house personnel or using an external consultant/agency.

Action Guidelines

1 How do I get a regular digest on overseas trade news, exhibition and trade fair information, government schemes, subsidies, etc.? *British Business* provides a weekly digest of news from the Department of Trade and Industry – an invaluable, up-to-date guide at £70.00 per annum.

   Contact
   British Business, Freepost, London SW1P 4BR.

Date contacted	Relevant	Not relevant
☐	☐	☐

2 Are there any specialist magazines/papers providing information on exports? *Export Times:* monthly news on all aspects of overseas marketing.

   Contact
   Export Times Publishing Ltd, 61 Fleet Street, London EC4.

Date contacted	Relevant	Not relevant
☐	☐	☐

   Export Direction: monthly news with good reader inquiry service and special features.

   Contact
   Export House, 20 Queensway, Enfield, Middlesex EN3 4SN.

Date contacted	Relevant	Not relevant
☐	☐	☐

3 How do I find out about international industry trends? *Predicasts/ Worldcasts* reports on new products, new capacities, product demand, end uses and sales.

   Contact
   local library.

Date contacted	Relevant	Not relevant
☐	☐	☐

4   How do I find out about market research which has been carried out?
    The International Directory of Published Market Research lists titles of
    research, countries/products covered and the date/source/price.

    Contact
    EMR Section, BOTB.

Date contacted	Relevant	Not relevant
☐	☐	☐

Findex lists 9000 reports from over 350 sources.

Contact
local library.

Date contacted	Relevant	Not relevant
☐	☐	☐

5   How do I find out about competitors, intermediaries and suppliers?
    Kompass; Dunn & Bradstreet; Yellow Pages.

    Contact
    local library.

Date contacted	Relevant	Not relevant
☐	☐	☐

6   How do I find out about overseas trade and professional associations?
    National Trade and Professional Associations of the United States,
    Columbia Books Inc. (1985), *Directory of European Associations*, CBD
    Research Ltd (1981).

    Contact
    local library.

Date contacted	Relevant	Not relevant
☐	☐	☐

7   How do I find out about overseas media? *Ulrich's International Periodicals Directory.*

    Contact
    local library.

    Date contacted   Relevant   Not relevant

8   How do I find out import and export figures for my products? *Overseas Trade Statistics of the UK*; Bureau of the Census, USA; foreign government statistics; OECD *Trade by Commodities.*

    Contact
    local library.

    Date contacted   Relevant   Not relevant

9   How do I find out about UK government statistics? *Guide to Official Statistics.*

    Contact
    HMSO, Atlantic House, Holborn Viaduct, London EC1.

    Date contacted   Relevant   Not relevant

10 How do I find out about future developments in overseas technology? The UK Patents Information Network provides early and detailed information on innovation and new technology.

    Contact
    Science Reference Library, 25 Southampton Buildings, London WC2A 1AW; or local library in network.

    Date contacted   Relevant   Not relevant

11
'Armchair' Exporting

- A high proportion of UK exports are handled by domestic organizations acting as intermediaries between local suppliers and overseas clients.
- They offer a low-cost, 'armchair' approach to winning export sales.
- 'Armchair' exporting can result in some loss of control in the way a firm's products are marketed overseas.

Introduction and aims

For the firm short on the resources, time and money necessary to open up export markets, the use of UK-based intermediaries is an alternative option. There are over 700 export houses operating in the UK, and it is estimated that 20% of export trade is handled by them. This unit describes how to gain access to export houses and other types of intermediary: many of them are located in London, and they carry out a wide range of export functions. Firms need to persuade them that they are worth representing – this requires a skilful and concerted selling approach. Although called 'armchair' exporting, this does not imply 'taking a back seat'.

> The southern-based representative of a steel stock-holding firm had been regularly calling on the London offices of the Crown Agents (who act on behalf of overseas principals), without success. Careful analysis of their buying structure revealed organizational changes in buyer responsibilities. The firm was not getting access to the right buying unit. Fresh approaches resulted in orders for Africa.

The following armchair intermediaries are examined:

- Subcontracting.
- Consortia.
- Crown Agents.
- Foreign buyers.
- Export houses.
- Export management companies.
- 'Piggy-back' exporting.

Subcontracting

The overseas links of most of Britain's larger concerns are such that the myriad firms supplying them are involved in exports. The goods are going overseas, albeit as parts of someone else's product. Subcontracting along these lines can be an appropriate strategy for a firm in the construction industry. A policy of identifying the architect, building concerns and consortia involved in and winning foreign orders, then using this as the basis of a contacts list, provides a route to significant subcontracting business.

Information note A regular and careful study of the press, both national and local, will highlight opportunities to subcontract. Organizations such as the Building Materials Export Group and the Royal Institute of British Architects publish lists of major projects and consultants, plus contractors/suppliers.

Subcontracting is not confined to the building industry. It plays a useful part in the export strategy of many smaller firms.

A small North-east rubber company has grown from less than 1% exports to almost 15% by identifying major projects/orders and taking on the short-run, difficult rubber work (at a premium price).

Consortia

These represent a major step down the road to direct involvement. The firm is participating in drawing up the approach to the market, providing its expertise to complement the specialized skills of the other members of the consortium. Recently, the Department of Industry has adopted a policy of encouraging combinations of smaller firms, even on the home market. These are frequently geared towards tackling specific projects, developing expertise in certain areas, or offering a broad range of potential customers. For example, suppliers of children's outerwear, children's socks and children's rainwear can link together to offer a more comprehensive range to overseas buyers. This smaller firm consortium route to exports offers considerable potential:

- It can minimize the costs for each firm.
- It can provide a range of expertise and resources that none would have individually.
- It offers customers a fuller product range, minimizing their buying and management costs.

A grouping of local craftsmen offered a wide array of hand-made traditional craft goods. They could therefore provide the customer group (US stores) with a wide array plus volume potential.

A group of textile firms targeted their efforts on the north European market. Each firm identified a manager with responsibility for relations with a specific customer group.

The Crown Agents

This is a non-profit-making organization which acts on behalf of numerous overseas governments and public authorities (but not for commercial concerns). The normal method of operation is to receive requests from a 'client' government to supply a particular item, line or tender for a project. The project is then put out for tender from known suppliers. It is important to get on the Crown

Agents' computerized list of potential suppliers and call regularly.

> **Contact point**
> Crown Agents, 4 Millbank, London SW1P 3JD (01-222 7730).

Foreign buyers

These act in broadly the same way as the Crown Agents but for commercial concerns. However, they take a large number of different forms, sharing the same characteristics of (1) being located in the producer's market and (2) placing orders in that market for an overseas organization. In their most simple form they are the wholly owned buying offices of certain large foreign department-store groups, e.g. Macy's, Sears Roebuck, Hertie GmbH (see *Stores of the World*, Newman Books Ltd (biennial)).

A number of firms exist which have been contracted to handle the purchasing for foreign buying groups. These independent buying houses offer access to some of the major names in world retailing, household names in their own countries and often in other countries. These concerns take an active approach to spotting and selecting new products and suppliers; they cannot afford the delay for new suppliers to contact them.

Although the bulk of the buying organizations mentioned above specialize in consumer goods and purchase for retail groups, a number of organizations dealing in industrial products purchase in the UK. Bear in mind that a prime (if not the primary) task of these buying organizations is to act as information gatherers. Only in exceptional circumstances do these bodies *place orders directly*. The home-based buyers are normally the decision-makers. Even when this route is adopted, therefore, a visit to the market can be a tremendous plus.

> A small knock-down kitchen manufacturer approached exporting through the UK buying offices but followed it up by a trip to America. Top management used the contacts established through the UK as their launching pad for a US visit.

Export houses

The last two approaches have involved the buyer coming to the market. Many firms use UK-based organizations, such as export houses, to take the firm's goods to the market. They are often experts on particular regions or specific customer groups. The most substantial firms are likely to be members of the British Export Houses Association (BEHA). These organizations operate in three main ways:

- As principals: buying in their own right, holding stocks, distributing and determining their own prices and promotional policies.
- With the manufacturer as principal: the producer retains ownership but the export house becomes his or her export department, handling procedures, documentation and selling (the precise balance is subject to negotiation).
- With buyers as principals: they buy for specific clients.

Over a forty-year period, a manufacturer of haberdashery items sold the bulk of its export output via a London export house. This long-term relationship did not prevent the export house seeking alternative suppliers as UK inflation forced up costs.

Contact point
BEHA, 69 Cannon Street, London EC4 (01-248 4444).

Export management companies

These companies can offer a range of services – from acting as the company's export department, and managing sales, documentation, shipment and finance, to offering sales expertise and contacts in specific market areas. Always ask them to substantiate their claims of contacts or business won. The simplest method is by asking them to put you in touch with some of their existing clients. Payment is usually based on a percentage of sales won, though a retainer is often required to cover development work and travel expenses.

'Piggy-back' exporting

Many larger concerns with established distribution channels in export markets are prepared to cooperate with smaller firms. Much depends on the complementary nature of the products and the benefits the larger concern will derive. The initiative to approach prospective partners often resides with the smaller firm, although specific opportunities may be advertised; ICI, for example, advertises its world sales network. But recognize that your exports are your responsibility; no one will do the job for you.

Summary

UK-based intermediaries offer a variety of services to small firm exporters providing 'armchair' access to world markets. Many of these services are provided on a commision-on-sales basis and so need not cost the firm a penny. Despite these advantages, there are drawbacks in dealing through UK-based intermediaries:

1 No contact with export customers.
2 Lack of control in the way products are marketed.
3 Little or no feedback information on export markets/customers.

Action Guidelines _____

1 Does the firm have an up-to-date contact list of architects, building concerns and consortia?

_____
_____
_____
_____

2 What ideas does the firm have on a local small firm consortium or linking up with a large local concern?

_____
_____
_____
_____

3 Has the firm made contact with:

- Crown Agents?
- Foreign buyers?
- Export houses?

 What was the result of these meetings? _____
_____
_____
_____
_____

4 What does this tell you about your export potential?

_____
_____
_____

5 If you have been approached by an export marketing company, have you:

- Obtained a detailed proposal? _____
- Taken up references? _____
- Come to an agreement on terms of payment? _____

_____

12
Getting the Most out of Agents and Distributors

- The appointment of an overseas agent or distributor is the beginning, not the end, of the export drive.
- Their effectiveness in the market rests on careful management, motivation and control.
- Working with agents/distributors leads to long-term commercial and legal commitments.

Introduction and aims

A market, a customer group or target industry, once chosen, requires a level of service to be established which will:

1 Win initial business.
2 Keep customer loyalty.
3 Provide a basis for developing a long-term presence in the market.

All at an affordable cost. At the centre of the effective servicing of customers is the recognition that their needs evolve from their domestic market circumstances, and the closer the firm gets to meeting these needs the more profitable the relationship. The use of agents and distributors can assist in this relationship and help achieve a greater 'closeness'. 'How do I get a good agent?' is probably the most common question asked by firms seeking to start off their exports, open up new markets or simply improve their export performance. Posed in this bold way, it begs two very important issues:

- Are good agents found or made?
- Do I need an agent anyway?

This unit argues that agency relationships are *made* by firms who work at them in a consistent and systematic way, and highlights ways forward in handling and managing them. Agency management is an integral element of the marketing effort to win export business and not a low-cost substitute for it. It may be true that an agent can open up a market despite the inefficiencies and indifference of the principal, but if he or she is the type of astute businessperson sought by most firms, he or she will recognize the inherent inefficiency of this and look for ways, including a search for new clients, to reduce this.

The agent's function

It has been estimated that agents handle over half the world's foreign trade. Despite the novelty of forms, the underlying role of an agent is *acting on behalf of another*. Once it is recognized that building exports through an agent demands hard work and active support – rather than the discovery of the much prized 'small hungry agent' who will do everything for the producer in return for his commission – then many owner/managers will naturally say: 'Why bother with agents anyway?' In the areas of component supplies to overseas export markets and processing, most customers prefer to deal direct. There is evidence to suggest that UK firms, notably industrial producers, use agents more than their foreign rivals and in situations where they may be inappropriate. The value of an agent depends on their potential contribution to opening up or developing a market. Low costs naturally play a part but any money saved is only one aspect of the real costs.

Agents provide local knowledge, some reassurance to customers, an on-going presence in the market, the scope for more frequent client contact, advice, information and the local's ability to work with buyers on their terms to the profit of both parties. At the same time, the requirements of the agent's own business may limit his or her ability to provide the technical expertise sought by some suppliers and purchasers in more technical product/service areas. The time scale involved in winning some types of business in these areas poses special problems for the agent. It can take years in the home market to open key accounts: the agent may be unwilling or simply lack the resources to get involved in this type of exercise.

There is no simple answer to the question: 'Do I need an agent anyway?' The firm has to think carefully through its needs for support in the market and the demands likely to be imposed by customers. In cases where an agent can meet both of these sets of conditions, then they have a role. Otherwise, it may be that the firm has to tackle the market direct or use some other type of intermediary. Success in handling agents and getting them interested in a product/service line involves four key elements:

1 Recruitment.
2 Management.
3 Motivation.
4 Control.

Recruitment of agents

Careful consideration at the recruitment stage lays foundations for secure future working relationships. Sloppy and indiscriminate approaches can create long-term problems.

> In Saudi Arabia, even preliminary negotiations or association with a disreputable agent can blight the whole venture.

Job description The most important first stage in any agency relationship is the drawing up of a clear job description.

> A Hull-based manufacturer of packaging machinery spent six months recruiting his first UK sales manager. This required

> working out a job description, gathering a short list and taking up references. Yet he appointed an exclusive agent to cover the whole of France following a chance meeting at a UK exhibition.

The aim of any recruitment and selection procedure, whether for internal personnel or agents, is to produce from a short list the candidate most capable of doing the job. The drawing up of a clear job description will establish its scope and dimension and specify the type of candidate best qualified and with the necessary experience to undertake the job. It should include the following features.

Type of agency The most common form is the commission agent. These represent their clients in return for the payment of a commission on sale. Commissions can vary considerably. They are used most efficiently for relatively low value products where frequent customer contact (related to the buying act) is necessary. Many commission agents are reluctant to accept projects involving considerable market development without hard orders, unless a fee to cover their 'investment' cost is agreed. The fee can be on a phased basis with commission taking over after a given development period. There are many types of agent and the exporter should consider all the possibilities, not just existing norms, and define the best type suited to the market and the requirements of the product.

Agency resources This will include the capabilities required to do the job effectively:

1. Location.
2. Telex facilities.
3. Size/turnover.
4. Growth record.
5. Number of sales personnel.
6. Sales calls per month.
7. Financial standing.

Agency capability The experience of the agent in the market, their degree of specialization, their contacts and their ability to provide orders are of prime importance. Other capability areas may include:

1 Technical specialization and competence to handle lines.
2 Experience in handling related or complementary lines.
3 Level of acceptance with trade/customers.
4 Knowledge of customs and import procedures.

The job description should be considered in very much the same way as the job description drawn up for an employee; as a mechanism of control and a basis for discussion. It should also be the foundation stone of any advertisement used to recruit agents.

Finding and choosing candidates Like any recruitment process, this calls for an array of strong candidates. For major manufacturers, this represents no great problem. Their reputation is sufficient to ensure a good sample from which to choose. Small firms need to treat this as more of a sales exercise. Field visits, research data and sales contacts provide valuable ammunition in the search for representation. Directed export activity speaks volumes about a firm's intentions and can persuade agents to come forward for interview. Other ways of building a short list for interview include:

Advertising in the market This is direct and positive but alerts competitors to your intentions. It can be expensive, and copy requires careful preparation.

Contacts The best recommendation for an agent comes from potential customers and the trade. In-market research may highlight names of potential agents, news of agency switches, principals dropping agents or key sales personnel leaving an established agency to set up their own independent operation.

Support services The BOTB, chambers of commerce, banks, industry and trade associations, etc. provide lists of potential agents. These lists lack a degree of selectivity and can often be out of date.

A Dutch textile agent interested in representing UK and other overseas suppliers registered with his local chamber of commerce.

> Following a successful career he moved out of that particular trade but continues to receive overtures from prospective firms circulated by a variety of agencies some twenty years later!

The BOTB has scrapped its agency finding service as too many companies simply wanted a short cut to orders without any effort. The service has been replaced by a wider 'market advisory service'.

Exhibitions An advertisement on the stand or in the exhibition handbook at both UK and overseas exhibitions may generate approaches. Agents identified through any of these channels ought to be cut to a manageable short list for interview.

During recruitment the following principles are paramount:

- *No agent should be recruited without careful evaluation.* Some firms will be unable to build up a satisfactory short list. Under these circumstances there is the temptation to appoint the best of a weak bunch in order to get active within the market. Agents recognized as mediocre or with little potential are unlikely to generate sales.
- *No agent should be recruited without a trial period of six or twelve months.*
- *Appointed agents should be willing to spend a significant period of time (say two weeks) at the producer's plant.*
- *Appointed agents should allow the producer to visit customers with them, on occasion.*
- *No manufacturer should fail to give the agent adequate support; visits twice yearly (minimum).*
- *Technical information, promotional support and involvement in pricing are also imperative.*

Management of agents

Certain facets of agent management have been covered in the final comments above. However, the dual role of the agent – part employee, part independent concern – should be kept constantly in mind. The key management skills here are:

1 Positive communication of targets and needs.
2 Fair and adequate remuneration.
3 Ensuring agents have the means to perform the tasks allotted to them.

In exporting (particularly for British firms), certain aspects of this support are essential, especially up-to-date, *accurate* delivery, quality and price information.

> 'I would not mind if they gave me longer delivery dates, so long as they kept to them. I have my other clients to think of. They become tarred with the same brush if I promise a customer a delivery date and it is not met' – disillusioned Dutch agent.

The management of an outside party who may represent other principals requires an understanding of the agent's needs and business objectives. It is often stated that the firm's major competitors in exports are not rivals but the other principals represented by its agent. The agent aims to promote his or her own business by offering to customers an optimum assortment of products/services which maximizes the commission payments and minimizes expenses. Over-emphasis on building new contacts or development work on one line disrupts this optimum mix. An agent's balanced portfolio provides the long-term security he or she requires to operate successfully. Rapid sales development disrupts the balance, and large commission payments may push principals to consider financing their own in-market selling operation.

Motivation of agents

This should be a combination of establishing incentives for action while ensuring that costs are controlled. One of the crucial elements in a high degree of motivation is *commitment* deriving from *involvement*. The agent must see the manufacturer as involved in his or her problems and committed to their mutual success. The simplest method of demonstrating this is through frequent contact and regular visits to the market. The good agent will want to service clients looking for long-term involvements in the market. Evolving product and promotional strategies which reflect that market's special needs satisfies both agents and end users. The agent ought to be permitted to play a role in this process, albeit within limits defined by the manufacturer.

Targets play a major part in both motivation and control. Involvement in the setting of targets is important for creating a high degree of motivation to succeed. The nature of agents as external, independent bodies increases the importance of this involvement. Simultaneously, agreement on marketing support – prices, promotion, product development – should be reached wherever possible. Targets are meaningful only to the degree that they (1) are achievable: too many firms expect too much from agents too early; and (2) meet the company's needs.

Exclusive or non-exclusive agents? Exclusive rights to handle products need not be handed over as a matter of course. National laws may directly affect this, but markets can be divided into sales territories which are offered to competing agencies. This can increase motivation and performance.

> A northern clothing firm managed key accounts and northern customers via its own sales force and used a network of five sales agents to cover the South of England. This same firm did not think twice about allowing a one-man agency the exclusive rights for the whole of West Germany.

Commission The late or irregular payment of commission and poor reward for effort is perhaps the greatest demotivator. Prior agreement on the following points is essential:

1 Amount of commission.
2 Currency in which commission is to be paid.
3 Dates of payment.
4 Any customers/orders outside of the agreement.
5 Cross-over payment, where two agents serve one transaction.
6 Any variances in the commission rate.
7 Promotional activity.

8 Development periods.

All these points should be carefully observed at regular review sessions.

Control of agents

Exporting is embarked upon to assist the firm's goals of profitability, security, growth, etc. A clear statement of these objectives and the required contribution of specific markets or agents ought to be drawn up by the firm (if only for internal discussion). This should provide the basis for agent control and the prime mechanism for control: *reward*. The firm's flexibility in agency relationships is constrained by existing market practice often backed by law.

> In Austria the conduct or actions of the two parties can constitute an 'implied agency' even if there has been no written or verbal agreement.
>
> All foreign firms selling goods in Oman are required to appoint an Oman company or individual as an agent. They must adhere to the Commercial Agency Law (CAL(1977)). These agencies must be listed in the commercial register, be members of the chamber of commerce, and have their principal place of business in Oman.

The performance of agents requires constant monitoring. The requirement to feed back in-market activities can frustrate a certain breed of agent.

> The West German agent for a rubber boat manufacturer regularly turned in the best sales figures. Yet he rarely sent written reports, which he found a waste of selling time.

Communication need not be one way. The exporting firm can regularly inform agents of:

1 Product changes.
2 New advertising material.

3 Other company successes.
4 The performance of other agencies.

This can be by telephone or telex rather than lengthy written reports.

> *Information note*   The Institute of Export has published a standard agency agreement, as has the CDH (German Association of Agents):
> 5 Koln 41 (Lindenthal), Geleniusstrasse 1, CDH-Haus, West Germany.

Many other countries have published standard 'selling' agreements. These are often available from their national chambers of commerce and industry or the joint chamber of the countries. In case of doubt contact the BOTB, whose country specialists will be able to advise.

Distributors

The key characteristics of the distributor are the ability to hold stocks and transport the goods around the market, and the willingness to tie up his or her own capital in the exporter's product. The distributor's investment provides an incentive to ensure buyer pull-through within the market. However, good distributors are probably harder to find than good agents. At the same time, their dual status as buyers – they frequently hold title to the goods – and distributors, or onward sellers, creates problems. The distributors' role as holder of stock, frequently with warehousing/wholesaling and even retail facilities across the country, is their great strength. It may create a situation where strong demands for support to ensure customer pull-through are made.

> 'We found a lot of specialist sporting goods distributors in the US willing to handle our goods but they wanted us to spend between $150,000 and $300,000 in advertising to support it. We haven't spent that in our entire history' – sports goods manufacturer.

Many distributors support their stock-holding set-up with sales and promotional activity. Their sales forces are frequently well equipped to expose the product to potential customers in many areas.

There is usually less call by distributors for exclusivity than with agents. In some markets there will be a principal distributor or agent-distributor, who acts as agent for transactions with the other distributors, normally for a commission. The principles of *recruitment*, *management*, *motivation* and *control* highlighted in the preceding discussion are particularly important here. The importance of support activities by the manufacturer, particularly home-based sales force activity, is recognized and required by most successful distributors.

Summary

The appointment of an overseas agent/distributor is an important decision requiring careful consideration. The appointment should be viewed as part of a long-term approach to building a presence in selected markets. Before appointing any form of representation, a clear picture is necessary of:

- Markets the firm wishes to develop.
- Structure, size and growth of the market.
- Support the firms can provide:
  (a) management back-up;
  (b) selling help;
  (c) production/stock-holding;
  (d) delivery times;
  (e) order acceptance/processing procedures;
  (f) product packaging/quality/warranty;
  (g) servicing;
  (h) returns and complaints procedures;
  (i) promotional and technical literature;
  (j) training.

Lack of definition and forethought can make the job offer unattractive to strong candidates. The job description forms the basis of the recruitment procedure.

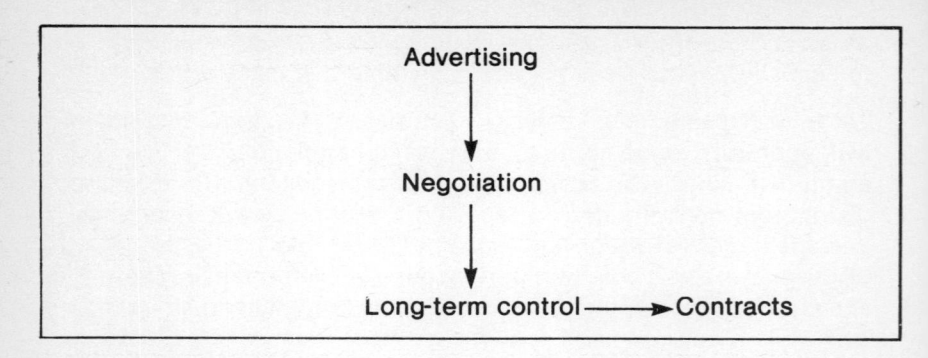

```
Advertising
    │
    ▼
Negotiation
    │
    ▼
Long-term control ──▶ Contracts
```

The job description will include: type of agency; agency resources; agency capability. Effective recruitment requires an array of strong candidates whose references are taken up – not chance meetings in hotel bars where exclusive rights to whole continents are signed away over the dry Martinis! It does happen. Be wary of the agent who collects principals like stamps but does not have the resources to service them effectively.

After recruitment, attention to *management*, *motivation* and *control* will help develop the full potential of the market for the firm's products and services.

Action Guidelines _____

Building an agency short list

1 Has the firm received inquiries from agents over the last two years?

   Details: _____
   _____
   _____
   _____

2 Approach contacts for lists of agents:

                                 Date   *Contact name*

   Banks
   Chambers of commerce
   International chambers
   BOTB – overseas post
   Industry or trade associations
   Agency federations
   Consultants

3 Has the firm contacted customers of related or complementary products for recommendations of local agents?

Contact	*Date*	*Outcome*
_____	_____	_____
_____	_____	_____
_____	_____	_____
_____	_____	_____

4 Consult:
   - Trade directories.
   - Yellow Pages.
   - *Kompass*.
   - Large firm financial accounts, which often list names and addresses of overseas agents/distributors.

Screening prospective agents

1 When was the agency founded?

   _____

2 Background of senior executives (education, experience, languages).
   _____
   _____
   _____
   _____

3 Details of other businesses they handle.

Name and address of principal	Referee	Turnover in market
_____	_____	_____
_____	_____	_____
_____	_____	_____
_____	_____	_____

4 Name and address of banker.
   _____
   _____
   _____
   _____

5 Referees checked.

Principals	Bankers	Date checked
_____	_____	_____
_____	_____	_____
_____	_____	_____
_____	_____	_____

6

Territory covered	Calls per month
_____	_____
_____	_____
_____	_____
_____	_____

7 Does the agency have:
   - adequate premises?
   - telex?
   - administration support?

- language ability?
- time to spend on new line?

8 Will the agency require other specialist facilities?

- Servicing?
- Design office?
- Proximity to accounts?
- Other?

9 Do you consider this candidate:

- very suitable?
- worth interviewing?
- reject?

Measuring performance of existing agents

1   Name of agents   Date appointed   Territory
    _____   _____   _____
    _____   _____   _____
    _____   _____   _____
    _____   _____   _____

2 Type of agreement/remuneration:
_____
_____
_____
_____

3 Contracts won during last two years:
_____
_____
_____
_____

4 Purpose of visits over last two years:
_____
_____
_____
_____

5   Results of visits (reports/action plans/memos):
    _____
    _____
    _____
    _____

6   Details of correspondence with agent over last two years:

    Telex: _____ Initiated by: _____
    Telephone: _____   _____
    Letter: _____   _____

7   Details of advertising and promotion material supplied:
    _____
    _____
    _____
    _____

8   Details of agency initiatives (e.g. symposium, exhibition, promotions):
    _____
    _____
    _____
    _____

9   How do you rate your agents?

Agent	Very effective	Adequate	Needs replacing
_____	_____	_____	_____
_____	_____	_____	_____
_____	_____	_____	_____
_____	_____	_____	_____

10 What can be done this month to improve the performance of the inadequate performer?

    Develop training programmes: _____
    Improved reward system/incentives: _____
    Improved communications: _____

13
Financing Exports

- Without payment for goods shipped, marketing efforts are wasted.
- Exporting entails greater risks of non-payment than domestic selling.
- Risks and complexity can be reduced and controlled by the use of external financial advisers.
- Astute financial and credit management supports a bold approach in taking on new customers and developing new markets.

Introduction and aims

Finance in its many forms plays a crucial role in ensuring profitability.

- *First* — In providing the pre-shipment finance to enable the company to produce the goods.
- *Second* — In providing effective methods for ensuring payment with the returns on which the firm has geared itself to operate.
- *Third* — In providing an adequate return over time for the risks taken and insurances adopted.

Modern exporting is further complicated by the problems of floating currencies creating an environment of risk where good business can dissolve into bad as currencies move relatively to each other. This unit describes the essential features of export finance and payment against this background of risk and returns. New exporters should not depend just on this outline but should always seek specialist advice.

Pre-shipment finance

Winning business anywhere costs money, and many of these costs are written into fixed overheads. It is sometimes possible to get payment in advance of production, but this occurs infrequently and the ensuing discussion presumes some post-delivery payment, e.g. 30, 60, 90 or 120 days net. During this period, the producer is considerably out of pocket for:

1. Business development.
2. Designs and developments (merely entering a tender can be a very expensive process).
3. Materials.
4. Machinery, time and any development work.
5. Tooling.
6. Labour.
7. Power.
8. Inventory.
9. Carriage, insurance and freight (or elements of this, depending on the trading terms).
10. Packaging.
11. Interest on money.
12. Any opportunity costs.

This is the negative part of the cash flow problem which hits many firms, particularly exporters. The classical method of 'paying off' these costs is through the margin earned on the business on payment and pre-shipment finance, deriving from previous business (assets) or overdrafts. All these costs bear some interest charges, either directly through overdraft interest charges, or indirectly through opportunity costs of capital.

Costs over time deriving from export business These costs, plus the interest chargeable on them, must be built into the pricing/return on investment policies of the firm. Failure to account properly for these developments can drastically reduce the apparent returns on export business (see Figure 21).

Sources of pre-shipment finance Most companies will set up to obtain overdrafts to cover these costs from their banks, normally on the basis of bank rate plus ½% to 2½%. Advances may be gained on the basis of ECGD cover. A company holding a suitable ECGD policy can apply for a banker guarantee to be given by the ECGD to the bank. Against this, the bank will advance money at preferential rates of interest. Where a banker's guarantee facility is not available, or ECGD cover is inadequate or difficult to obtain, the firm may enlist the assistance of *confirming houses* or *factors*.

Confirming houses 'The essential function of a confirming house is to reaffirm, as a principal, orders placed by an overseas buyer.' This means that the confirming house carries the risks of non-payment instead of the seller. The manufacturer will normally find that this means it can treat the export order virtually as a domestic sale. Confirming houses will generally advise on sources of credit. Payment will normally be cash against documentary proof of delivery of goods f.o.b. In their normal sphere of operations the confirming house provides these services to the buyer.

Factors These provide financial services to manufacturers wishing to relieve themselves of the problems of carrying credit. The factor purchases invoice debts from the manufacturer at a discount and can turn orders for goods into immediate cash – usually 80% of the value of the invoice with the balance paid when the money is collected. They normally offer a purely financial service with no involvement in documentation or selling. It is advisable to ensure that all finance arranged through factors is on a non-recourse basis. For this service, exporters will have to pay between 2½% and 3½%, which may be less than setting up and managing a credit control facility, and collection may be quicker. These costs must be built into export prices.

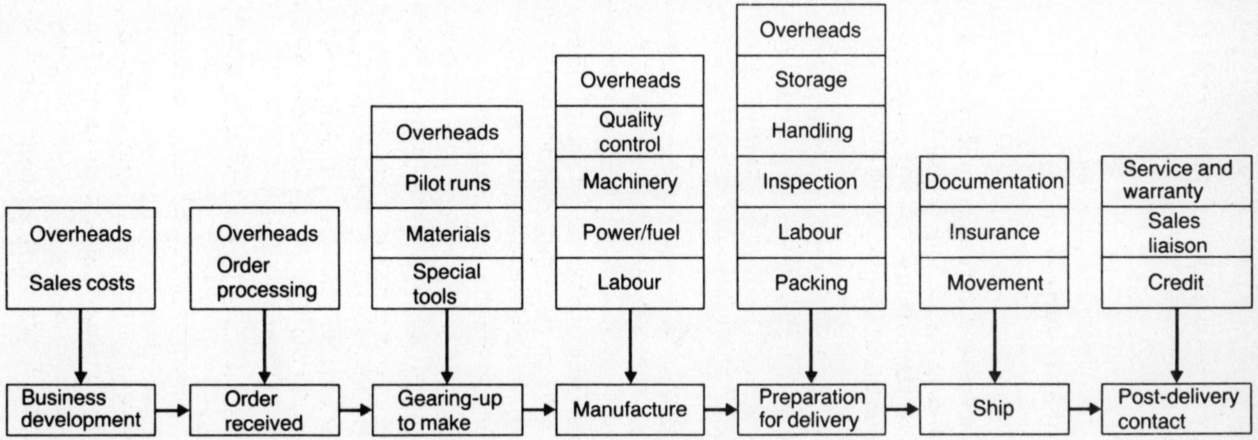

Overheads	Overheads	Overheads	Overheads	Overheads		Service and warranty
Sales costs	Order processing	Pilot runs	Quality control	Storage	Documentation	Sales liaison
		Materials	Machinery	Handling	Insurance	Credit
		Special tools	Power/fuel	Inspection	Movement	
			Labour	Labour		
				Packing		

↓ ↓ ↓ ↓ ↓ ↓ ↓

Business development → Order received → Gearing-up to make → Manufacture → Preparation for delivery → Ship → Post-delivery contact

Figure 21

Contact point
The Association of British Factors, 11 Bolt Court, Fleet Street, London EC4A 3DU (01-353 1213).

Post-shipment finance

Credit terms can be a major element in securing export orders. There are no hard and fast rules about credit periods. Although this might generally be longer/shorter in some markets, it remains part of the total contract and hence subject to negotiation. *Clear definition of terms is absolutely necessary.*

Methods of payment offer considerable scope for discussion but will inevitably be the subject of negotiation: *always discuss these at length with the company's financial advisers and banker.* The three prime alternatives are:

1 Cash with order Here the buyer extends credit to the supplier. This is a rarity; more common is the payment of a cash deposit with the balance paid either by (a) *open account* – although common in domestic trading, goods dispatched and payment made against invoice, it is relatively unusual in exports; it normally occurs when a long-standing business relationship has been established – (b) *cheque* –

'A small mail order retailer exporting goods to the USA at an order value of $20–$60 accepts personal cheques drawn on US banks as the usual method of payment. Cheques are paid into a US bank account and funds repatriated periodically, so that the £1.21 charged by a UK bank for negotiating each US dollar cheque is spread over a worthwhile sum. So far no cheque has been returned unpaid.'

Source: *Journal of the Institute of Export*, vol. 47, No. 2, March 1984, p. 22, by permission of the editor.

– or by (c) *banker's draft* – a cheque drawn by the buyer's bank which is sent to the exporter who in turn obtains payment via his or her own bank – or by (d) *mail or telegraphic transfer* – the buyer's bank instructs a correspondent bank to credit the exporter's account with sterling or foreign currency; a telegraphic transfer speeds up the process.

2 Bills for collection This involves dispatching the goods and sending the shipping document to the firm's bank for onward transmission to the importer's bank. The importer is informed of the conditions under which he or she will be able to obtain the documents and hence the goods, usually on payment or acceptance of bills of exchange. This system provides more security than open account and the exporter can sell the bills for cash at a discount.

3 Documentary letters of credit 'A documentary credit is an instrument by which a bank undertakes to pay a seller for his or her goods providing he or she complies with the conditions laid down in the credit.' This means that the seller is assured of payment *provided that all conditions are met*, and the buyer is protected from paying if irregularities occur. The basic procedure involves:

(a) The conditions for the letters of credit are agreed between the exporter and importer.

(b) The importer requests his or her bank to open a credit in favour of the exporter.

(c) The exporter is then advised of the credit through a bank in his or her own country, usually but not always his or her own bank. *The exporter should then carefully examine the terms and conditions. All must be met before payments are made.*

(d) After payment or acceptance, the documents are sent to the importer's bank for processing and on to the importer enabling him or her to take possession of the goods.

Simplifying export finance for the smaller firm

For firms with a small or intermittent export trade, some new bank schemes are designed to simplify post-shipment financing, e.g. the Midland Bank International Smaller Exports Scheme. These schemes have the following advantages:

- Finance provided is over and above annual borrowing limits.
- Takes away the administrative burden of dealing with ECGD.
- Simple procedures.
- They charge 1½% over base rate and will advance up to 90% of the amount outstanding.

Export Credits Guarantee Department (ECGD)

Information note The points made here are abstracted from *Insurance Facilities of the British Government's Export Credits Guarantee Department*, prepared by the Export Credits Guarantee Department and the Central Office of Information. This should be obtained.

The ECGD is a self-financing department of HM Government offering a selection of services geared to protect exporters from some of the financial risks of exporting. The ECGD is the 'only organization in this country which insures exporters and those financing export credits against political and exchange transfer risks as well as commercial (default or insolvency) risks'. The ECGD covers a significant proportion of Britain's overseas trade, covering areas as diverse as consumer goods, engineering components and capital equipment. Consultation with ECGD officers will highlight the policy best suited to the needs of each specific exporter. These policies fall under four broad headings:

- Insurance for supplier credit.
- Guarantees for supplier credit financing.
- Guarantees for buyer credit financing.
- Cost-escalation, performance bond, consortium insurance, insurance for overseas investments.

These are described in detail in the ECGD booklet mentioned above. The policy most commonly used by small firms is *the comprehensive short-term guarantee*. This is a continuous guarantee subject to annual renewal, providing cover for non-payment in the case of:

1   Insolvency of the buyer.
2   The buyer's failure to pay within six months of accepting the goods.
3   Failure to take up dispatched goods by the buyer.
4   A general moratorium on external debt decreed by the government of the buyer's country.
5   Action by the government of the buyer's country preventing performance of the contract in whole or part.
6   Political, economic, legislative or administrative acts occurring outside the UK delaying or preventing payment.
7   Legal discharge of debts in a foreign currency resulting in shortfalls at the date of transfer.
8   War and certain other events preventing performance of the contract.
9   Cancellation or non-renewal of a UK export licence or the prohibition or restriction on the export of goods from UK by law.

Although this is a continuous guarantee, for large sums, credit limits may be imposed by ECGD for specific buyers. These policies cover up to 90% or 95% of the losses involved. Premiums are established on the basis of a flat rate per £100 of contracts covered.

In building up its services, ECGD has established an extensive dossier on the credit-standing of overseas buyers to assist in determining the nature and extent of cover.

Sales covered by the 'comprehensive short-term guarantee' can be financed by the banks at preferential terms through direct bank guarantees. For a small additional premium, ECGD provides unconditional guarantees of 100% repayment to banks. This enables the bank to lend on highly preferential terms.

Summary

Export finance and credit insurance are a large and complex area in which specialized expertise is necessary and, fortunately, widely available. This unit has reviewed specific aspects, but certain areas – such as for forfeiting, the role of the merchant banks and the problems of foreign exchange – are not covered. It is important to search out advice and, on occasion, shop around for these and the other financial services mentioned in this unit. This will alleviate problems in raising capital to finance exports.

Action Guidelines _____

1 Can the firm draw on its own resources to finance exports?
   _____
   _____
   _____

2 Is the firm making the best use of export finance?
   _____
   _____
   _____

3 Does the firm have an ECGD policy?
   _____
   _____
   _____

4 Has the firm considered alternative methods of financing exports, e.g. factors, small firms exporter schemes?
   _____
   _____
   _____

5 How efficient are the firm's credit control procedures?

   Very efficient The firm knows exactly where customers stand and new customers are vetted quickly: good liaison between credit control and sales.

   Efficient The firm knows exactly where customers stand, but new customers are not vetted quickly; some conflict between credit control and sales.

   Inefficient Lack of up-to-date information on credit standing; customers are vetted so slowly that the firm loses the business.

6 What remedial action is to be taken on credit control?
   Action:_____
   _____

   By whom: _____
   When: _____

14
Administration for Exports

- Complete, accurate and properly processed documentation is essential.
- Freight forwarders are able to handle much of this work.
- If handled internally, more systematic and computerized methods have overcome the burdens associated with documentation.

Introduction and aims

Administration problems, particularly the time consumed, the complexity of arrangements and worries about documentation, represent some of the most common barriers to small firms considering exporting. A survey by the North of England Development Council (NEDC, *Export North*, Newcastle, 1976) noted that:

- 25.7% of small firms did not export because it was too time-consuming.
- 8.6% did not export because it was too complex to organize.
- 51.1% felt that they needed more help on exporting techniques and documentation.

Although these problems are very real, solutions to all of them exist and the entire process can be handled by even the smallest company. This can be managed through using organizations and approaches geared to reducing the demands on scarce resources:

- Selecting markets carefully.
- Using intermediaries where possible.
- Using travel agents specializing in business travel.
- Employing freight forwarders.

Certain facets of administration, particularly *documentation*, require clarification, although there are many organizations set up to provide this service, normally at a very small cost. The majority of companies can use freight forwarders or documentation agencies to handle all documents apart from those which must be completed by exporters themselves:

1. Commercial invoices (see Figure 22).
2. Packing lists where they do their own packing (see Figure 23).
3. EUR 1.*

These key documents provide the starting point for a series of carriage, insurance and freight documents. Many smaller firms find that their involvement in the documentation process can be kept to a minimum in the early stages of exporting. As their business grows, involvement tends to develop in parallel. The basic elements of the documentation process are:

1. The contractual terms.
2. The trading process; carriage, insurance and freight.
3. The payment conditions.

These will be outlined below. It is important to recognize the importance of Britain's membership of the EEC in this process. From the industry's Brussels nomenclature, through to the Community Transit (CT) System, membership is influencing the terms and conditions of trade.

---

*Movement certificate EUR 1 is required for goods claiming EEC preferential rates of duty. Approved exporters can be issued with pre-authenticated forms by Customs.

The contractual terms

The vast bulk of international trade takes place under the set of international rules titled *Incoterms 1953* (revised 1967 and 1974). A copy of *Incoterms* should be obtained from either the International Chamber of Commerce, the local chamber of commerce or the Institute of Export. These *Incoterms* exist to provide a uniform set of rules to avoid misunderstandings and misinterpretation. They cover the main aspects of business contracts. They determine exactly what is implied by the major types of agreements to supply and the obligations of the buyer and seller in each circumstance.

Ex-works The seller makes the goods available, at the factory gate, bearing all costs of packing, loading on to 'conveyance provided by buyer', and supplying necessary documents.

Free on board (f.o.b.; f.o.b. airport) The seller agrees to deliver the goods on board the vessel and meet all associated costs and obligations up to that point.

Cost and freight (C&F named port of destination) The exporter meets all costs involved in shipping the goods to a named port of destination, providing all necessary licences, authorizations and clean, negotiable bills of lading.

Cost, insurance and freight (named port of destination) The exporter meets all charges of carriage, licensing, loading and insuring the goods up to a port of discharge, also to provide a clean bill of lading, invoices and insurance policies.

Delivered duty paid (d.d.p. named place of destination in the country of destination; duty paid) The seller agrees to meet the costs and complete arrangements to put the goods and associated necessary documents at the disposal of the buyer at an agreed destination, usually the buyer warehouses or plant.

The precise terms and conditions are the subject of negotiations between the parties and should be absolutely clear before any action to deliver is made. Each partner in the contract will recognize differential advantages in specific arrangements.

Figure 22

INVOICE	FACTURE FACTURA	RECHNUNG FACTUUR		
Seller (Name, Address, VAT Reg. No.)				C.C.C.N No.
	Invoice No. and Date (Tax Point)		Seller's Reference	
	Buyer's Reference			
Consignee	Buyer (If not Consignee)			
	Country of Origin of Goods		Country of Destination	
	Terms of Delivery and Payment			
Vessel/Aircraft etc.	Port of Loading			
Port of Discharge				
Marks and Numbers; Number and Kind of Packages; Description of Goods			Gross Weight (Kg)	Cube (M3)

Specification of Commodities	Quantity	@	Amount (State Currency)
		TOTAL	

Name of Signatory

Place and Date of Issue

Signature

It is hereby certified that this invoice shows the actual price of the goods described, that no other invoice has been or will be issued, and that all particulars are true and correct.

380-2

© SITPRO OVERLAYS 1983 V2

Figure 23

LISTE DE COLISAGE
ESPECIFICACIÓN DE EMBALAJE
VERSANDLISTE

PACKING LIST

Exporter/Shipper (Name and Address)	UK Customs Reference/Status		Sheet No.
	Invoice No. and Date (Tax Point)		Exporter's Reference
	Buyer's Reference		Other Reference(s)
Consignee	For Official Use		
Marks and Numbers; No. and Kind of Packages; Description of Goods		Quantity	Other details

SITPRO OVERLAYS 1981

See Principal Sheet for further details of this Consignment

> Buying houses from overseas store groups frequently prefer to buy ex-works as this permits them to complete their own container loads. Many European buyers are pressing for all terms to be on the basis of *delivered* costs.

Many of the specific trading documents refer directly to these terms. However, in cases of problems occurring, the International Chamber of Commerce provides an Arbitration and Conciliation Service.

The trading process: associated documents

The major export documents are as follows.

The invoice Detailing the goods (type, quantity) and money payable, plus details of any freight or insurance costs. *All contracts require an invoice in some form which must be completed by the exporter.* Goods for certain countries have to be invoiced on specially prepared *consular invoices* which can be obtained from the consul of the country concerned. The invoice will detail your Customs Cooperation Council Nomenclature (CCCN). This enables customs to identify goods for statistical, duty or clearance purposes. Contact HM Customs and Excise to obtain the correct CCCN. A pro forma invoice is used for making quotations and is headed with the words 'Pro Forma'; it can be used to obtain payment where the buyer has agreed to pay in advance.

Certificates of origin These specify points of origin of goods and are required for certain countries, particularly where preferential duties exist for UK goods. These are issued by organizations designated by national governments: in the case of the UK, chambers of commerce affiliated to the Association of British Chambers of Commerce – *required only for certain items in specified countries.*

CT system These are forms used in the EEC to provide evidence as to whether or not the goods are in free circulation (entitled to duty-free or reduced intra-community duties). The main forms are

T2 and T2L. The CT system reduces border formalities by using one transit procedure for the whole of the EEC.

Bill of lading This is one of the most important documents in international trade, as it is the document of title to the goods which are the subject of contract between buyer and seller. It serves many purposes, being:

1 Contract between shipowner and shipper.
2 Receipt for goods received.
3 Transferable document of title, required by importer to clear his or her goods on arrival.

The importance of the bill of lading means that the conditions described in it must be strictly adhered to. 'Clean' bills of lading are required for most contracts identified under *Incoterms*. This means that no superimposed clauses recording defective conditions of goods or packings exist. Bills of lading will normally include details of shipper, vessel, consignee, terms of carriage, method of identifying goods, ports of discharge, dates and timings. The bill of lading will normally specify whether freight is payable or paid (see Figure 24).

Airway bill This takes the place of a bill of lading, but does not provide title to goods.

Rail and road consignment notes/truck and carrier receipts These are receipts for goods and are issued by rail authorities or road hauliers. They cannot be used to prove title to goods, but merely indicate to whom the goods are dispatched.

Customs declarations Exporters or their forwarders complete a declaration form for presentation to Customs and Excise before shipment. The most common is form C273. Alternatively, the new Simplified Clearance Procedure (SCP) allows firms to register in advance and receive a Customs Registered Number (CRN). This allows firms to export and not submit an export declaration for fourteen days.

ATA carnets This is an international customs temporary importation document providing a relatively simple procedure for

Figure 24

BILL OF LADING

DART CONTAINERLINE

B/L No.

Shipper		
Consignee (If 'Order' state Notify Party and Address)		
Notify Party and Address (leave blank if stated above)		
Pre-Carriage by*	Place of Receipt*	
Vessel	Port of Loading	
Port of Discharge	Place of Delivery*	
Marks and Nos; Container No:	Number and kind of packages; description of goods	Gross Weight	Measurement

Freight details, charges etc.

RECEIVED by the Carrier for shipment on the vessel named herein or substitute for carriage between the port of loading and the port of discharge by the said vessel and by any other vessel or vessels or other means of conveyance to which transhipment may be made in the course of the voyage and/or for arrangement or procurement of pre-carriage from place of receipt and on-carriage to place of delivery where stated above, the goods as specified above in apparent good order and condition unless otherwise stated. The goods to be delivered at the above mentioned port of discharge or place of delivery, whichever applicable, on payment of outstanding freight or charges thereon. Subject always to the exceptions, limitations, conditions and liberties set out on the reverse side hereof, to which the merchant agrees by accepting this B/L.

In WITNESS whereof THREE (3) original B's/L, if not otherwise stated below, have been signed by the Agents on behalf of the Carrier one of such B's/L being accomplished the other(s) to be void.

Ocean Freight Payable At	Place and date of Issue
Number of Original Bs/L	
Shipped on board the	

*Applicable only when document used as a Through Bill of Lading.

PARTICULARS DECLARED BY SHIPPER

importing goods for:

1 Trade fairs.
2 Commercial samples.
3 Professional equipment.

These cover all EEC member states plus a number of other countries. The firm may obtain the carnet on depositing a percentage of the value of the goods or a guarantee plus a fee with an issuing chamber of commerce.

TIR carnets Outside of the CT systems, these provide for sealed vehicles to travel from customs offices or departure points (where sealing takes place) to their destination, without further examination or payment of customs duties in each country *en route*. Carnets are issued and guaranteed by the Road Haulage Association.

Insurance When the exporter accepts responsibility for the insurance cover for his or her goods, a major additional responsibility is accepted. Normally, regular exporters alleviate the problems by adopting an overall policy. The most common form of policy in force today is the Lloyd's SG (Ships and Goods) Policy. This will cover all risks mentioned, describe the consignment and provide details of transferability and currencies involved.

Test and quality assurance certificates In many product fields (e.g. cars, caravans, electrical equipment) differing technical standards exist throughout the world. Test certificates may be required to provide evidence that the units meet the specific requirements of the market. A number of industry research associations (e.g. the Motor Industry Research Association) have the facilities and authority to provide tests and certificates for products destined overseas.

Simplication of International Trade Procedures (SITPRO)

The need for some system of simplifying export documentation has long been recognized by the major trading nations. Britain has made significant progress in this direction through the development of a series of aligned commercial documents for export under the auspices of the SITPRO Board. The foundation stone of the aligned system is the *master document* which contains all the information required for the succeeding aligned forms. With the master document as the basis, the

1   shipping note;
2   consignment note;
3   export cargo instrumentation;
4   bill of lading;
5   certificate of insurance;
6   HM Customs Entry 273;
7   EUR 1;
8   invoices;
9   dangerous goods declarations;
10 Arab-British Chamber of Commerce certificates of origin;
11 community transit forms;

can be extracted from a combined use of photocopies and acetate overlays.

This system provides for the completion of only one export document by the manager and the mechanical copying of a large number of other parts from this (see Figure 25). The advantages of this system lie not only in the saving of time and money, but in the much greater accuracy – assuming the master document is completed properly.

Summary

Administration, particularly documentation, is one of the greatest barriers to small firms entering exports. A judicious use of external organizations and a growing familiarity with procedures as business develops can overcome these real problems.

Figure 25

Disc 37 Job 46844a

MASTER DOCUMENT

© SITPRO 1981

Start

Exporter	Vehicle Bkg. Ref.	Customs Reference/Status		Tariff Heading
	Invoice No. and Date	Exporter's Reference		
	Buyer's Reference	Forwarder's Ref.		S.S. Co. Bkg. No.
Consignee (If 'Order' State Notify Party and Address)	Buyer (If not Consignee)			
	Name of Shipping Line or C.T.O.			Port Account No.
Freight Forwarder	Country of Consignment	COUD	ICD	Container	ToT	Flag	Port
	Country of Origin of Goods	Country of Final Destination		
	Terms of Delivery and Payment			
Receiving Date(s)	Dock, Container base Etc.			
Pre-Carriage by	Place of Receipt by Pre-Carrier			
Vessel/Aircraft Etc.	Port of Loading	EUR 1 or C. of O. Remarks		
Port of Discharge	Place of Delivery by On-Carrier	Insured Value (state Currency)		Name of Receiving-Authority
Marks, Nos. and Container No.: No. and Kind of Packages; Description of Goods (For Dangerous Goods Specify Correct Technical Name; Hazard Class; UN Number; Flash Point °C)		Tariff/Trade Code Number	Gross Weight (kg)	Cube (m³)

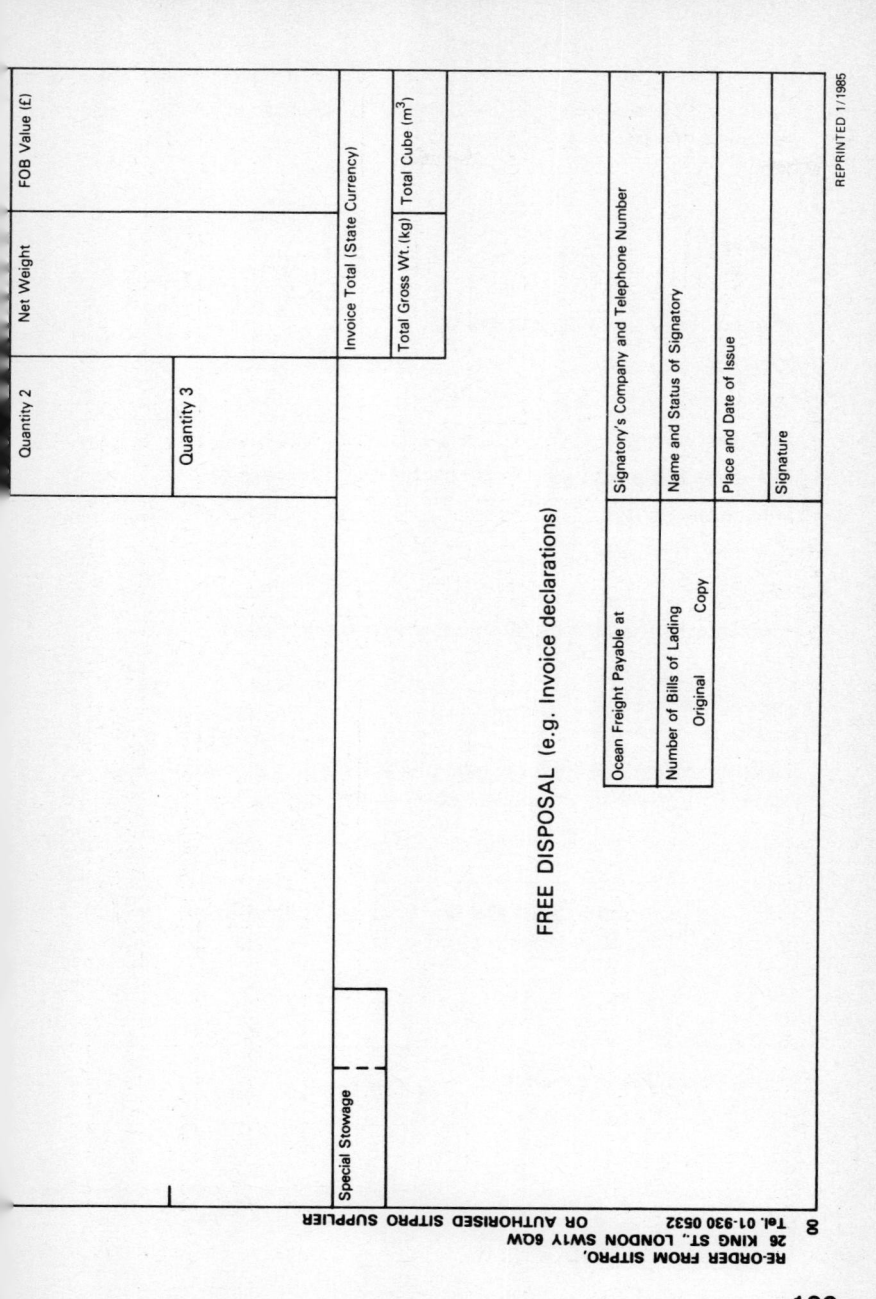

Quantity 2	Net Weight	FOB Value (£)
Quantity 3	Invoice Total (State Currency)	
	Total Gross Wt. (kg)	Total Cube (m³)

Special Stowage

FREE DISPOSAL (e.g. Invoice declarations)

Ocean Freight Payable at	Signatory's Company and Telephone Number
Number of Bills of Lading Original Copy	Name and Status of Signatory
	Place and Date of Issue
	Signature

REPRINTED 1/1985

RE-ORDER FROM SITPRO,
26 KING ST., LONDON SW1Y 6QW
Tel. 01-930 0532
OR AUTHORISED SITPRO SUPPLIER

8

199

Action Guidelines _____

1. How does the new exporter propose to handle export administration and procedures?

   Internal:

   External:

2. What will be the result in terms of:

   Costs?_____

   Efficiency?_____

   Customer service?_____

3. How does the existing exporter perform in the areas of:

   Order processing?_____

   Order monitoring?_____

   Dispatch? _____

4. How trouble-free is completed export documentation?

   Over 80% correct   ☐
   Over 60% correct   ☐
   Over 40% correct   ☐

5. Has the firm reduced export administration costs and improved customer service over the past year? If not, why not?

   _____
   _____

6. What remedial action does the firm propose to take to improve the efficiency of export administration?

Action	When	By whom
Staff training	_____	_____
Subcontract documentation	_____	_____
Introduce SITPRO system	_____	_____
Improved internal communications	_____	_____
Other	_____	_____

15
Communicating with Overseas Markets

- Relations with overseas customers are reinforced by a programme of effective communication.
- Regular communication reassures customers and keeps them informed and up to date.
- Sales inquiries from overseas need to be handled in the same way as domestic inquiries.

Introduction and aims

In the search for new business overseas, firms are obliged to communicate with the market which is made up of:

1. end users;
2. customers;
3. intermediaries;
4. business publics;

to inform them of what products and services are on offer and how they can meet changing needs more effectively than existing suppliers. Methods include letters, telephone, telex and personal visits. Once business links are established, continued communication is essential in reassuring customers and intermediaries of the firm's ability to continue to supply at the right time and the right service levels. Too often, UK firms are criticized for losing interest in the market, and for not having the tenacity to overcome objections; where sales are to be won there is a lack of persistence and follow-up.

This unit outlines how firms can create a favourable climate for their products and services by regular and clear communications.

Letter contact

Initial contact with potential customers and agents will probably be by letter, and as business develops letters will form a major method of communication. A neat and consistent letterhead and easy-to-understand details of post codes, telephone numbers – with full international dialling codes – and telex numbers make communication simpler. Letter inquiries demand a prompt and courteous reply.

> A Dutch importer/distributor circulated a number of UK manufacturers of training and soccer shoes, expressing interest in a 'tie-up'. A prompt reply and invitation to discussions by an East Midlands firm impressed the Dutch firm and eventually led to an agreement. Very few firms bothered to reply to the letter.

Promptness is an impressive characteristic. When it is a hallmark of early business dealings it can help overcome the anxieties many markets still harbour about UK firms' ability to deliver.

Using the phone

The telephone is the most direct, prompt and positive way of communicating with the market. Many firms are intimidated by the prospect of using the phone, whether to follow up a sales inquiry from the west coast of the USA or chase up an agent in West Germany who has gone 'quiet'. Similar situations within the domestic market are immediately followed up by a call, and, in the case of a sales inquiry, a request for more information, checking of references and a call for a meeting. In the export market, inquiries can take many weeks to answer, as there may be translation problems and doubts about the seriousness of the inquiry. A reply when formulated usually goes out in letter form, in a defensive and often unhelpful style. An immediate telephone call can solve many of these problems, but remember:

- Get the full dialling code.
- Check on time differences.
- Prepare the points you wish to cover.
- Speak slowly and clearly.
- Don't get flustered when the telephonist answers in a strange language.
- Take notes.
- Confirm the conversation by telex or letter.

Where travel funds are limited, regular use of the telephone keeps the firm in touch, lubricates the relationship, reassures customers and motivates agents.

A rubber moulder supplying overseas export markets had also developed a number of in-house products with application in the fire-fighting sector. A one-man West German distributor had placed some orders but for some months had lodged no progress reports and had not responded to written requests for information. Orders were sporadic and arrived with little warning. This created production scheduling difficulties. The 'marriage' was going through a rough patch. The distributor did respond to a series of personal calls which helped inspire confidence, and a forward order schedule for the year arrived in the post.

The appointment of a telephonist/receptionist with language ability will assist the importing/exporting firm requiring regular overseas telephone contact. If this is not possible, ensure that personnel receive adequate training in developing a polite, consistent and understandable telephone manner.

Telex contact

Few investments will pay better dividends to the serious exporter than a telex, particularly when the firm is involved in long drawn-out negotiations, and where products exported have a high technical content. Where cost precludes the purchase of a telex machine, the shared use of a local number (which can be inserted on the firm's letterhead) should be considered. This service is supplied by local export clubs, chambers of commerce and commercial secretarial companies.

Personal visits

Getting out and into the market is at the heart of practical efforts to communicate. In the owner-managed firm, the owner is very much the firm, and can sort out problems on the spot and make decisions. Without regular visits the firm is operating in the dark. Even when business is developing smoothly it is important to visit the market regularly, not just as a 'flag-waving' effort. Visits require:

- Proper planning.
- Objective setting.
- Writing up in a report form.
- Following up action points.

Assistance in the planning of an itinerary can be obtained from a local travel agent. They will help with transportation and hotel reservations, advice on visas, vaccinations, etc., and obtaining the most economic rates. Remember to shop around, as travel services vary in quality. When planning an overseas trip, check that:

- The local post is informed well in advance of your visit.
- Passport is valid.
- The visit does not clash with local holidays, holy days, etc. (see the BOTB's 'Hints to Exporters' series).

- Appointments are confirmed.
- The visit does not extend to more than two weeks (beyond that the executive is unlikely to be effective).
- Opportunities perhaps exist for linking the visit with an outward mission: this reduces costs and trip organization.

Summary

Close attention to prompt, consistent and regular communication are important when (1) responding to overseas inquiries and (2) building business overseas. The basic elements of international communication are:

1 Letter.
2 Telex.
3 Telephone calls.
4 Personal visits.

Communication is complicated by distance, language and cultural differences; but customers and agents, whether in Manchester, Dusseldorf or Bergen, need to be informed and reassured.

Action Guidelines _____

1. What is the turn-around time for responding to overseas inquiries?

    _____
    _____
    _____
    _____

2. How does this compare to performance within the domestic market?

    _____
    _____
    _____
    _____

3. How often does the firm contact its overseas customers and agents?

    Every week?
    Every month?
    Every six weeks?

4. What methods are used? (Check copy correspondence.)

    _____
    _____
    _____
    _____

5. Does the firm set overseas trip objectives, e.g.

    - develop new customers?
    - introduce new products?
    - carry out market research?
    - motivate local sales agents?
    - resolve specific problems?

    _____
    _____
    _____
    _____

16
Managing Overseas Promotion

- Special attention to promotion helps the company build a sustainable position in export markets.
- The allocation of funds for promotion should be jointly agreed and managed with local intermediaries.
- The well-defined target audience attending trade fairs makes such fairs one of the most cost-effective forms of promotion.

Introduction and aims

UK firms are criticized for emphasizing low price as a way into export markets and neglecting the non-price factors of promotion, distribution and product. Each factor must play its part in order to sustain export business, but it is promotion which prepares the ground and creates the necessary climate for the firm or its appointed agent to sell. In this unit, we will examine the components of promotion which support and stimulate sales, and how careful and creative management can stretch a limited promotional budget for maximum effect. The major components are:

- Trade fairs.
- Publicity.
- Literature.
- Advertising.

Establishing the budget

'How much should be spent on export promotion?' is a question often asked. There is no single answer to fit every situation, but it should be viewed as a key component of marketing strategy, not as a luxury to be given up when export sales or profits decline. There are four main methods commonly used in deciding the size of the budget:

What can I afford? This approach continues to treat promotion as a luxury and results in a fluctuating promotional effort.

Percentage of sales This sets promotional budgets on the basis of export sales turnover: it is simple to implement and helps firms control expenditure. But the approach can be short-sighted and can lead to violent fluctuations just at a time when increased promotional efforts are crucial for reviving export business.

Competitor marketing Spending according to competitors is a defensive rather than a pro-active approach. In many instances exporting firms will not be able to match the spending of locally based competitors. Firms attempting to service a wide range of export markets will find promotional budgets spread so thinly they can make little impression against local competition.

Market objectives The most rational approach is allocating promotional expenditure in accordance with in-market objectives, i.e. 'What are we trying to achieve with our promotional efforts, and what are the costs of achieving this?'

Trade fairs

Overseas trade fairs provide an attractive opportunity to get a snapshot picture of a market or trade and as such are particularly useful for the start-up exporter. Over a few days competitors, customers, end users and distributors are crammed under one roof, presenting opportunities to:

- Sell.
- Build leads.
- Introduce new products.
- Support local agents/distributors.
- Carry out marketing research.

In reality, many firms bungle the opportunity and publicly display their ineptitude and lack of professionalism for all to see, treating the event like a seaside outing rather than a critical part of the firm's export promotion efforts. Proper planning makes the difference between success and failure, and for overseas exhibitions this requires:

- Objective setting.
- Selecting from among alternatives.
- Project planning and organization.
- Follow-up and evaluation.

Objective setting Firms considering exhibiting need to establish clear objectives. Attractive BOTB subsidies or the fact that the competition have taken space are not sufficient reasons for booking space. Exhibitions, despite subsidies for the less experienced exporter, are expensive affairs consuming considerable management time, money and anxiety. From the outset, realistic objectives should be set and 'woolly' reasoning rejected. Like all good objectives they should be quantified, e.g.

- To attract 80% of existing customers on to the stand.
- To open 10 new accounts.
- To attract 25 end users on to the stand.
- To obtain 20 good quality sales leads.

The objectives should then be communicated to other members of the firm who will be manning the stand. Quantified objectives will make evaluation simpler and help direct future changes in promotional policy.

Selecting from among alternatives Exhibitions and trade fairs are a growth business and there are a host of venues competing for custom. They may be local, regional, national or international in scope. It is important that the firm compares what is available with objectives rather than simply taking advice from a local agent or continuing to exhibit because the firm has always taken space. Some of the major UK exhibitions such as the Boat Show and IFE are international in outlook and attract many overseas buyers.

Henri Lloyd Ltd of Manchester, who produce quality specialized waterproof clothing for the outdoor leisure trade, yachting, mountaineering, and rambling, attended the *Daily Express*-sponsored International Boat Show in January 1964 as a start-up company with *no* customers. By the end of the exhibition, they had opened ninety accounts throughout the UK and received serious inquiries from Europe. A follow-up trip generated orders from four European countries. Exports now account for 50% of sales.

Exhibition organizers provide audited data on attendance records and visitor profiles.

Contact point

Incorporated Society of British Advertisers, 2 Basil Street, London SW3 1AG (01-584 5221).

Also by obtaining the exhibition handbook and contacting listed participants, the firm can get a clearer indication of relevance and suitability. First time round it is worth considering attending as a visitor. The firm can still access decision-makers and buyers as well as check on competition – all without the added burden of organizing a stand. Contacts made can always be interviewed at a 'hospitality suite' in a local hotel. What happens if there are no exhibitions in the firm's specific area of activity or they are not capable of meeting company objectives? It may be worth considering a mobile exhibition to get products to the doorstep of specific target customers.

> A northern upholstery company uses a mobile exhibition van to promote products to key UK accounts. It is viewed as convenient by UK buyers. The van was used as a cost-effective and direct method of promoting the firm, its products and its serious intentions about exports to Europa-Mobel of Belgium.

Project planning and organization In planning an exhibition it is important to consult the BOTB as there may be a collective presentation of UK goods and services under the sponsorship of a trade association or chamber of commerce. For 1985/86 a first-time exhibitor can obtain stand space at 45% of the cost, and this can be further reduced by sharing small stands of more than 15 sq m with firms in a complementary or supporting area. The extra marketing 'clout' of the collective presentation is an added benefit to the smaller concern.

Given the lead-in time to the exhibition, details of any subsidies and the fact that every recognized exhibition offers a shell scheme as a way of reducing costs and removing one area of planning, the firm is ready for the detailed project planning:

- Establishing an exhibition budget: this should cover the stand, transportation, hotels, pre-event publicity, entertainment.
- Stand design: provide a clear brief based on exhibition objectives to a specialist display designer. Small extras, such as coat hooks during winter months, refrigerators to keep drinks cool during the summer, and ample display lighting, make all the difference.
- Preparing and briefing stand personnel: where there are language difficulties, local interpreters can be hired on the day at a very reasonable rate (in West Germany, 100–150 DM per day).
- Attracting customers to the event.
- Arranging transportation and clearance of exhibits. Advance application to chamber of commerce for ATA carnet.
- Arranging staff accommodation: at popular exhibition centres, like Cologne, Paris and Dusseldorf, accommodation is booked up to two years in advance.

Is all this worthwhile to set up a shop window in Paris or Utrecht? Many firms fail to realize that exhibiting has become a complex three-dimensional exercise in promotion and advertising which, if carried out effectively, can generate substantial benefits. Long-term planning cannot ensure success but it can help avoid trade fair disasters such as arriving on the eve of the exhibition to find stand exhibits have got stuck in customs. On the day, stand personnel need to be briefed and a rota system of breaks established; standing all day can be a tiring business. Rules on smoking, drinking, attire, etc. need to be established and adhered to. Adequate literature and methods of recording information about potential customers are prerequisites.

Follow-up and evaluation Following up inquiries and converting them into sales are the key to effective exhibiting. Interest fades rapidly after an exhibition closes, and tardy follow-up is no good for the customer or the company. Finally, the exhibition results should be compared to original objectives, and costs compared to benefits. Spending on exhibitions rather than other forms of promotion or advertising requires justifying. Critical evaluation enables the firm to carry out this exercise.

Overseas publicity

For the firm short on funds, publicity is an attractive way to reach a waiting public. If handled in a consistent and professional manner, it generates free exposure and sales leads. Publicity can be more believable than advertising and, for the firm used to issuing press releases in the UK, this practice should be extended overseas. The ground rules remain the same:

- Build mailing list of relevant journals, periodicals, newspapers, etc. with named contacts.
- Develop consistent format – letterhead, contact name and address.
- Type double-spaced on A4, with wide margins.
- Use short sentences; don't be vague or make extravagant claims.

- Answer the questions raised by 'who', 'what', 'where', 'when', 'why' and 'how'.
- Illustrations will always help a news story.
- Use a headline.
- The release must be newsworthy.
- Translate press release into the recipient's language.
- Beating the patriotic drum will not impress overseas editors.

It is worth circulating newsworthy stories to internal members of staff as a way of building good employee relations and maintaining company backing for the export initiative.

The Central Office of Information helps firms to publicize newsworthy products and services. They write and translate press stories and arrange for selective distribution overseas. If the news is suitable for use in other media such as radio, films or TV, it is passed for the consideration of the media division concerned.

Certain managers have specialist areas of know-how. When linked with a good writing style, this can be used to promotional effect by producing feature articles for technical journals.

The managing director of a North-east electronics engineering company produced a feature article for *Wireless World*, some copies of which found their way into the West German market. A researcher from Siemens was interested in the technical issues raised in the article. A meeting followed, and now Siemens is the major export customer for the firm's components.

Another useful press service is supplied by EIBIS International Ltd. The 26,000 journals and newspapers of the world have been listed and analysed into 366 subject categories and seven market areas. For instance, in the area of fire fighting and fire prevention, EIBIS has identified 31 related journals in Western Europe, 13 in Britain and Ireland, and 3 in Australia, New Zealand and South Africa. EIBIS offers a press story production and translation service to UK exporters at reasonable cost.

> **Contact point**
> EIBIS International Ltd, 3 Johnson's Court, Fleet Street, London EC4A 3EA (01-353 5151).

> A UK manufacture of ship's cranes used EIBIS to publicize its products in Australia. This resulted in seven inquiries interested in manufacturing locally under licence.

Literature

The exporter's catalogues, brochures and leaflets are a major material link with intermediaries and customers. Designing and printing literature for a number of export markets is an expensive operation, due to origination costs of design work, photography and typesetting. The job can be left to the local intermediary, but the exporter loses control of the message and production quality. A more sensible approach is to split the costs down the middle, with both parties vetting and agreeing copy and design. Standard UK literature will create a poor impression overseas: local language literature is the accepted norm. Don't skimp on translation costs, but always use a professional and preferably a resident of the target country. Catalogues and brochure copy should major on how product use will *benefit* the customer, rather than be a listing of product features. Remember, good literature should:

1 Be market-specific.
2 Be of good quality.
3 Communicate a message and inform.
4 Stick to the theme.
5 Push benefits.

Advertising

Advertising is often beyond the budgets of many small firms and yet it is one of the most powerful promotional tools. Many agents and distributors will push their principals to invest money in advertising in order to help build awareness and generate sales. Decisions on advertising strategy and expenditure can be delegated to the intermediary, but a shared approach is likely to yield better results.

Summary

Promotion is the company's attempt to stimulate sales. Its function is to inform and persuade: to inform potential export customers that the company is active in the market with its individual products and services; to persuade customers of the superiority of those products/services over competitive offerings; and to create a desire for purchase. It is not enough to rely on low price and the efforts of a local intermediary to build business. The components of export promotion – trade fairs, publicity, literature and advertising – have a separate but complementary impact, and it is the responsibility of the exporter to coordinate these components into a promotional campaign.

Action Guidelines _____

1 Describe the firm's domestic promotional activities over the last year.
   _____
   _____
   _____
   _____

2 Can any of these activities be modified for the export market?
   _____
   _____
   _____
   _____

3 On the scale 5 (a lot) to 1 (not at all), assess how the following promotional elements can aid your export selling effort:

	5	4	3	2	1
Publicity in technical press					
Publicity in regional press					
Publicity on TV					
Publicity on radio					
Local demonstrations					
Exhibitions					
Mobile exhibitions					
Symposia					
Seminars					
In-store promotions					
Newspaper advertising					
TV advertising					
Radio advertising					
Film advertising					
Literature					

4 Draft the firm's export promotional campaign for the next six months.

Month	Advertising	PR	Exhibitions	Literature	Other
1					
2					
3					
4					
5					
6					

17
Planning for Exports

- Effective managers increase the proportion of their time spent on planning as their enterprises expand.
- The export marketing plan helps mobilize the resources of the firm and matches them against identifiable export opportunities to provide a clear sense of purpose and direction.
- Translation of export plans into action is a measure of an enterprising organization.

Introduction and aims

Any small firm's owner-manager venturing into a business school library in search of some fresh insights into how to improve business performance will be overwhelmed and surprised at the sheer volume of book titles which include the words 'strategic', 'policy', 'long-term' and 'planning'. Despite the proliferation of academic writing it cuts little ice with the small firm manager: the major barrier is expressed in the view, 'With the best will in the world, the formulation of detailed plans today will not result in immediate action to help shift the increasing pile of stocks in the front yard or resolve the high reject rate or win export business.' In other words, planning may be an interesting theoretical exercise, but it has little impact on, or relevance to, the pressing problems of today, and is therefore rejected, or its implementation is postponed until operational problems are under control. Recession has exacerbated this negative attitude towards planning, as the managing director of a small southern-based bedding manufacturer found:

> 'Who could have forecasted and planned for the slump in demand which hit my industry? Now more than ever I have to remain flexible and quick to respond to the market. I can't be tied down to any plans or objectives; only a desire to survive and quick, seat-of-the-pants decisions will see me through.'

This comment reflects the typical small firm view of planning that it is a strait-jacket restricting the intuitive flair and responsiveness of the small firm to meet changing customer needs. Who can find cause to blame this attitude when many large firms have been inept in grasping the real purpose of planning and have muddled the issue, whilst others have hidden behind complex mathematical models very often irrelevant to the small firm? In many small firms there is little written communication, with reliance on informal word-of-mouth contact. However, growth via exports demands the understanding and skill to apply fundamental management principles, and the commitment of pen to paper. It need not involve specialist mathematical techniques requiring massive injections of time, planning, skills, data and increased staffing, but management by hope is not enough in the complex world of international markets. It requires a hard-nosed planning approach to reduce uncertainty and make the best use of scarce resources and demands:

- The ability to stand back from the day-to-day business of getting things done and reflect on what needs to be done.
- The ability to plan and set realistic objectives for export market development.
- The vision to develop an organization structure responsive to the requirements of export markets served.
- The ability to adopt long-term horizons on planning, market and profit development.

This unit provides a planning framework which will help the firm:

1. Match resources with export opportunities.
2. Set and achieve realistic export objectives.
3. Develop a consistent export marketing strategy.
4. Build an organization capable of servicing export markets.

Getting started

The most difficult thing about planning is getting started. Few managers would deny the inherent logic of planning for the future development of the business, but the problem is getting away from the short-term issues and problems which constantly demand attention. Rather than address this planning issue alone, try to set up a 'workshop' involving the rest of the management team and a trusted outside adviser. Schedule the session outside of normal working hours, at a venue away from the office and the interruptions of daily office life. Circulate an agenda a week or two beforehand with a number of broad headings, but stress that the purpose of the workshop is to collect positive contributions, information and ideas which can be hammered into a working plan. Use a flip chart and a black felt-tip pen to record contributions and comments and act as a focus for the workshop group. Keep the style of the session creative, positive and forward-looking: steer well away from criticisms of past failure. The check-lists in the preceding units can be completed individually and then compared together by members of the workshop group. This will provide a rich data base covering:

- Purchasing and licensing objectives and strategy.
- Export experience.
- Top management commitment.
- Export resources.
- Export network.
- Export opportunity selection.
- The support services as an extra resource.
- Export market information.

- Methods of export market entry.
- Financing exports.
- Export marketing options.

Setting objectives

Given the resources available, it is important to enunciate just what the company is trying to achieve so that the whole export programme is given direction and drive. Objectives are end results to be achieved, not wishful thinking. To help close this gap between wishful thinking and achieved results, it is helpful if objectives are:

1. *Arrived at through participation* by all those directly involved in achieving them; the 'workshop' approach provides an ideal vehicle for management to discuss the agreed export objectives.

2. *Few in number* rather than many, and written down specifying quantities and target dates; some of the items that should be included in detail are:
   (a) target sales of product/by unit and value (f.o.b./c.i.f.);
   (b) target market share by product;
   (c) target number of agents/distributors;
   (d) target contribution/profitability;
   (e) research activities to be completed.

3. *Changed as market conditions change* – planning is not a strait-jacket, and it would be ridiculous to pursue an export sales objective for Poland following that country's placement on the ECGD black-list.

4. *Consistent with domestic objectives* – objectives are formal statements on *what* the firm wants to achieve in export markets. If this is locked inside the owner-manager's head, nobody will know how well the company has performed by year end. They need to be written down and referred to: objective setting is the motor of the export planning process.

Export strategy

Strategy planning is deciding *how* the firm will achieve its export objectives. In earlier units we explored exports as one of a number of corporate strategic options in the search for growth. Export business strategy outlines broadly how management sees the firm achieving export objectives. It emerges from an appraisal of the best way of taking the company forward to achieving these in a coherent way. Clarity and succinctness pay off here. Put another way, strategy is the art of using and committing available resources to achieve objectives. Strategies should be changed in relation to opportunities and changes within export markets, but constant changes mean a company does not have strategies – just confusion. Strategic options include:

- Market concentration – concentrating resources in key targeted areas.
- Product development – constantly developing and augmenting products and services on offer to export markets.
- Market spreading – gaining a small market share in an array of export markets.
- Short-term profit.
- Long-term growth.

Action plans

So far, so good. Now comes the difficult bit:

> *Converting plans*
> *into*
> *actions*
> *which get results.*

This is the problem of integrating the disparate actions of the business behind the main objectives. What is required is regular communication by meetings, company publications, training programmes and briefing everyone about the export objectives and strategy of the business – getting everyone singing from the same hymn sheet and moving in the same direction. Once the main objectives and strategy have been established, individual members of the firm can develop their own action plans to help achieve the agreed-upon objectives. These too should be put in writing. This will provide a basis for discussion and improve coordination. Of critical importance here are actions to be taken concerning the management of the marketing programme:

1 Pricing.
2 Product.
3 Promotion.
4 Distribution.

Plans which take into account the full range of marketing actions open to the firm are more likely to provide results than a concentration on, say, low prices or an insensitive cost-plus pricing approach. Action plans should be consistent with overall strategy.

Budgets and controls

Funds need to be set aside specifically to achieve objectives and to facilitate action. It is no good lumping export activities under general budget headings. Similarly it is worthless planning for exports when there is no financial underpinning to resource the effort. Individual action plans require regular monitoring – not as a negative control mechanism but as a positive method of helping people achieve objectives.

Summary

The export plan can be condensed into a couple of sides of paper and should be referred to daily as a working document: 'Is what I am occupied with today in line with stated objectives?' However, the key benefit of planning is not the written plan but the process of thinking through the future development of the business which goes on long after the written plan has been produced.

Action Guidelines _____

1 Detail the firm's major export strengths and weaknesses.

Strengths	Weaknesses
_____	_____
_____	_____
_____	_____
_____	_____
_____	_____
_____	_____

2 How do your colleagues view the firm's major export strengths and weaknesses?

Strengths	Weaknesses
_____	_____
_____	_____
_____	_____
_____	_____
_____	_____
_____	_____

3 What are the firm's export objectives over the next year?

_____
_____
_____
_____
_____
_____
_____
_____
_____

4 State the overall export strategy to be adopted in achieving these goals.

   _____
   _____
   _____
   _____
   _____
   _____

5 Indicate the alternative strategies and the reasons for their rejection.

   _____
   _____
   _____
   _____
   _____
   _____
   _____

6 Detail individual action plans.

	Action	By whom	When
Price	_____	_____	_____
Product	_____	_____	_____
Distribution	_____	_____	_____
Promotion	_____	_____	_____

7 List budgets to support these actions.

Appendices

1 Export groups and councils

Book Development Council
19 Bedford Square
London WC1B 3HJ
tel. 01-580 6321

British Agricultural Export Council
35 Belgrave Square
London SW1X 8QN
tel. 01-245 9819

British Association of Used Plant Exporters
Byeways
Horsenden Lane
Princes Risborough
Nr Aylesbury
Bucks HP17 9NE
tel. Princes Risborough 5710

British Consultants Bureau
Westminster Palace Gardens
1–7 Artillery Row
London SW1P 1RJ
tel. 01-222 3651

British Food Export Council
6 Catherine Street
London WC2B 5JJ
tel. 01-836 6593

British Health-Care Export Council
28/30 Market Place
London WC1N 8PH
tel. 01-580 7912/7915

British Knitting Export Council
16–21 Sackville Street
London W1X 1DE
tel. 01-734 6277/8

Building Materials Export Group
33 Alfred Place
London WC1E 7EN
tel. 01-636 6920 telex 261446

Clothing Export Council
26 Sackville Street
London W1X 2QT
tel. 01-434 1881 telex 25149

Export Council for the British Jewellery and Giftware Federation
St Dunstan's House
Carey Lane
London EC2V 8AA
tel. 01-606 0871

Export Group for the Constructional Industries
3 Dean Trench Street
Smith Square
London SW1P 3HD
tel. 01-222 0323

National Wool Textile Export Corporation
Lloyds Bank Chambers
43 Hustlergate
Bradford BD1 1PE
tel. Bradford 24235/6

2 British Overseas Trade Board regional offices

1. **North East**
   Stanegate House, 2 Groat Market
   Newcastle upon Tyne NE1 1YN
   tel. 0632-324722

2. **North West**
   Sunley Building, Piccadilly Plaza
   Manchester M1 4BA
   tel. 061-236 2171

3. **Yorkshire and Humberside**
   Priestley House, Park Row
   Leeds LS1 5LF
   tel. 0532-443171

4. **West Midlands**
   Ladywood House
   Stephenson Street
   Birmingham B2 4DT
   tel. 021-632 4111

5. **East Midlands**
   Severns House
   20 Middle Pavement
   Nottingham NG1 7DW
   tel. 0602-506181

6. **South West**
   The Pithay, Bristol BS1 2PB
   tel. 0272-272666

7. **South East**
   Ebury Bridge House
   Ebury Bridge Road
   London SW1W 8QD
   tel. 01-730 9678

8. **Scotland**
   Alhambra House
   45 Waterloo Street
   Glasgow G2 6AT
   tel. 041-248 2855

9. **Wales**
   Cathays Park
   Cardiff CF1 3NQ
   tel. 0222-824171

10. **Northern Ireland**
    IDB House, 64 Chicester Street
    Belfast BT1 4JX
    tel. 0232-233233

3 COI regional offices

Birmingham
Five Ways House
Islington Row
Birmingham B15 1SH
tel. 021-643 8191 telex 337576

Bristol (South Western)
Government Buildings
The Pithay
Bristol BS1 2NF
tel. Bristol 291071 telex 44203

Cambridge (Eastern)
Three Crowns House
72–80 Hills Road
Cambridge CB2 1LI
tel. Cambridge 58911 telex 81187

Leeds (Yorkshire and Humberside)
10th Floor
City House
New Station Street
Leeds LS1 4JG
tel. Leeds 38232 telex 55472

London (London and South Eastern)
Atlantic House
Holborn Viaduct
London EC1N 2PD
tel. 01-583 5744
telex for London Region 264513

Manchester (North Western)
22nd Floor, Sunley Building
Piccadilly Plaza
Manchester M1 4BD
tel. 061-832 9111 telex 337576

Newcastle upon Tyne (Northern)
Andrews House
Gallowsgate
Newcastle upon Tyne NE1 4TB
tel. Newcastle upon Tyne 27575
telex 53277

Note The Northern Ireland Information Service, the Scottish Information Office and the Welsh Office Information Division act as agents for the COI in Northern Ireland, Scotland and Wales respectively. Addresses as follows:

Northern Ireland Information Service
Stormont Castle
Belfast BT4 3ST
tel. Belfast 63011 telex 74163

Scottish Office Information Division
New St Andrews House
St James Centre
Edinburgh EH1 3TD
tel. 031-556 8400 telex 727301

Welsh Office Information Division
3rd Floor
Oxford House
Cardiff CF1 2XG
tel. Cardiff 44171 telex 49327

4 International chambers of commerce

Australia
Australian British Trade Association
32 Bougainville Street
Manuka
Canberra (PO Box 141 Manuka)
ACT 2603 Australia

Austria
British Trade Council
Peter Botham Esq OBE
Mollwaldplatz 1
1040 Vienna
Austria

Belgium and Luxembourg
British Chamber of Commerce for Belgium and Luxembourg
30 Rue Joseph II
1040 Brussels
Belgium
tel. (02) 2190788

Brazil
British Chamber of Commerce
Head Office:
Rua Barao de Itapetininga 275
7th Floor, Caixa Postal 1621
Sao Paulo
Brazil
tel. (011) 0519

Rio Office:
Rua Real Grandeza 99
22281, Rio de Janeiro
tel. (021) 226 0564

Canada
British Canadian Trade Association
Suite 202, 10 Kelfield Street
Rexdale
Ontario M9W SA2

Chile
British–Chilean Chamber of Commerce
Agustinas 972
Oficina 1011
Casilla 536
Santiago, Chile
tel. 85266

Colombia
Colombo–British Chamber of Commerce
Cra 10 Nos 15–39, Piso 10
Apartado Aereo 4305
Bogotá
Colombia
tel. 234 79 21

Denmark
British Import Union
Borsbygningen
Copenhagen K
Denmark
Denmark DK-12-17

Finland
Finnish–British Trade Association
Etela Esplanaoi 2
00130 Helsinki 13
Finland

France
British Chamber of Commerce France (INC)
6 Rue Halévy
75009 Paris
France
tel. Paris 073 63-40

Germany, Federal Republic of
British Chamber of Commerce in
Germany
Heumarkt 14
5000 Köln 1
Federal Republic of Germany
tel. (0221) 238655

Greece
British–Hellenic Chamber of
Commerce
4 Valaoritou Street
Athens 134
Greece
tel. Athens 3620 168 3635 683

Indonesia
Indonesia–British Association
c/o PO Box 2159/JKT
18 Jalan Gajah
Mada
Jakarta

Israel
British–Israel Chamber of
Commerce
126–134 Baker Street
London W1M 1FH
tel. 01-487 5908

Israel–British Chamber of
Commerce
2nd Floor
Bank Hapoalim BM
104 Hyarkon Street
PO Box 61034
Tel Aviv
Israel
tel. Tel Aviv 240144 telex 32111

Italy
British Chamber of Commerce for
Italy
Via Tarchetti 1/3
20121 Milan
Italy

Japan
The British Chamber of Commerce
in Japan
PO Box 2145
World Import Mart Branch
Tokyo 170 Toshima-Ku
tel. 03 987 1620

Malaysia
The British–Malaysian Industry and
Trade Association in Kuala Lumpur
PO Box 2574
Kuala Lumpur KL23-07
Malaysia

Mexico
The British Chamber of Commerce
and Trade Centre
Rio Tiber 103
6th Floor
Colonia Cuahtemoc
Mexico 5 DF

Middle East
Arab British Chamber of Commerce
42 Berkeley Square
London W1X 5DB
tel. 01-629 1249 telex 22171

Morocco
British Chamber of Commerce for
Morocco
291 Boulevard Mohammed V
Casablanca
Morocco

Netherlands
Netherlands–British Chamber of
Commerce
Javastraat 96
2585 The Hague
Netherlands
(also offices in London and
Manchester)
tel. (8070) 468888

New Zealand
British Trade Association of New Zealand INC
Commerce House
126 Wakefield Street
Wellington
New Zealand
(PO Box 11363)

New Zealand United Kingdom Chamber of Commerce and Industry (NZUKCCI)
6th Floor
Dorland House
18–20 Lower Regent Street
London SW1Y 4PW
tel. 01-930 2524

Nigeria
Nigerian–British Chamber of Commerce
131 Broad Street
PO Box 109
Lagos
Nigeria
(also 69 Cannon Street
London EC4N 5AG)
tel. 01-248 4444

Norway
British Business Forum
c/o British Embassy
Thomas Heftyesgate 8
Oslo 2
Norway

Portugal
British–Portuguese Chamber of Commerce
Rua da Estrela 8
Lisbon 2
Portugal

Singapore
Singapore International Chamber of Commerce
Denmark House
Singapore 0104

South Africa
South Africa–Britain Trade Association Ltd
433 Union Centre
55 Harrison Street
Johannesburg (PO Box 10329)
South Africa

Spain
British Chamber of Commerce in Spain
Marques de Valdeiglesias 3
Madrid 4
Spain
tel. (91) 221 9622

Sweden
British–Swedish Chamber of Commerce
Nybrokajen 7
111–48 Stockholm
Sweden
tel. (08) 20 95 70 telex 10838

Switzerland
British–Swedish Chamber of Commerce in Switzerland (INC)
Dufourstrasse 51
8008 Zurich
Switzerland
tel. Zurich 05 32 30 60

Thailand
British Chamber of Commerce in Thailand
Bangkok Insurance Building
302 Silom Road
Bangkok
Thailand

Turkey
British Chamber of Commerce of
Turkey (Association)
PO Box 190
Karaköy
Istanbul
Turkey

Turkish–British Chamber of
Commerce
Avon House
360–6 Oxford Street
London W1N 9HA
tel. 01-491 4636 telex 28800

USA
British–American Chamber of
Commerce
275 Madison Avenue
New York, NY 10016
tel. 212-889-0680

British–American Chamber of
Commerce and Trade Center of the
South West Pacific
Suite 562
The World Trade Center
333 South Flower Street
Los Angeles
California 90017
tel. 622-7124-213

San Franciso British–American
Chamber of Commerce and Trade
Center
68 Post Street
Suite 714
San Francisco
California 94104
tel. 397 0250-451

Uruguay
Uruguayan–British Chamber of
Commerce
Avenida del Libertador
Brig. Gral. Lavalleja 1641
ESC 201
Montevideo
Uruguay
tel. 90-06-36

Venezuela
Cámara Venezolano Britanica de
Comercio e Industria
Edificio Blandin
Piso 1, oficina 1c
Chacaito
Apartado 5713
Caracas
Venezuela
tel. 32-44-93 and 33-20-09

Index

Abecor 99
action guidelines
  administering exports 200
  'armchair' exporting 158
  commitment 58–60
  communications 206
  export experience 47–49
  export resources 72–73
  financing exports 184
  growth options 27–28
  market research 149–151
  planning 223–224
  promotion 216
  purchasing and licensing 39–40
  selecting opportunities 111–112
  using agents and distributors 171–174
  using commercial services 140
  using Government agencies 128
  using the network 82–85
Advance Lubrication Services 94
advertising, *see* promotion
  Incorporated Society of British Advertisers 210
  shared advertising 215
agents, agency for agents 163
  action plans 221-2
  capability 162–163
  commission/fees 162, 166–167
  communication 168
  control 167
  evaluation 164
  exclusivity 166
  federations 171
  German Association of Agreements 168
  job description 161
  law 122, 167
  management 164, 173–174
  motivation 165–166
  portfolio 165
  recruitment 122, 161–163, 171
  references 172
  selection 163, 171–172
  targets 166
  typology 162
Airway bill 193
American Machinist Journal 133
annual reports 78
Association of British Factors 179
audit-resources 66, 73
autoclave firms 55
awareness 14

banks 80, 99, 119, 129–131, 177–180
  charges 179
Barclays International Report 55
Barclays Mercantile Factoring 130
Benns Exporters' Year Book 104
bills of exchange 180
bill of lading 193, 194
Birmingham Chamber of Commerce & Industry 135
  British business – Department of Trade & Industry Publications 121, 149
British Export Houses Association – BEHA 156
British Importers Confederation 34
British Overseas Trade Board –BOTB 16, 24, 65, 67, 79, 107, 114–123, 226
  briefing BOTB 114–117
  building relations 117–118
British Standard BS5 179 35

British Standards Institution (BSI) 68, 137, 145
Building materials export group 106, 153
bureaucratic inertia 51
buyer credit 131
buyers – multinational 78
buying houses 80, 155, 192

capacity 62–63
Carnet – ATA 135, 193, 196, 211
carriers receipts 193
cash flow 67, 176
catalogue of contacts 76, 80, 94
Central Office of Information – COI 123, 213, 227
certificate of origin 192, 197
chambers of commerce 80, 135–136
  international chambers of commerce 136, 228–231
  clothing firm 15, 32–33, 94–95, 166, 210
coal and log effect gas fire firm 45
commitment 41–42, 50–57
  underwriting commitment 60
communications 201–206
  telephone contact 202–203
  telex contact 80, 204
competitive activity 45, 54
competitive evaluation 104–106
concentration on key markets – BETRO Report 110
conciliation service 192
Confederation of British Industry 134
confirming houses 177,
  see also finance
consignment notes 193
  goods 130
consortia 154
contractual terms 187
conveyor belt firm 104
cost and freight, C & F 187
cost, insurance and freight, CIF 187
country profiles – BOTB guide 118
craft firm 154
crane firm 214
credit control 184

Croners Reference Book for Exporters 104
cross-licensing 36–37
Crown agents 152, 154–155
currency fluctuations 40
customer complaints 28
customs and excise 34, 99, 124, 192, 193, 212
  declarations 193

databases 145
delegation 54
delivered duty paid, ddp 187
Department of Health & Social Security 80, 123
desk research 33, 142–146
Development agencies 138
'Devils advocate' to improve business 28
differential advantage 74
diplomatic post 204
Directory of British Associations 134
distribution 152–174
distributors 36, 168–170
  see also agents
diversification 24
documentation 185–200

economic evaluation 97–104
EIBIS 213–214 see publicity
electronics firm 213
emergency lighting firm 79
engineering firms 23, 24, 32, 43, 43, 44, 52, 54, 119–120, 132–133, 139
enterprise agency 138
equestrian firm 43
European economic community 102, 192
  community transit system 192–143
exclusivity see agents
exhibitions and trade fairs 133, 164
  evaluation 212
  mobile exhibitions 210
  on the day 212
  project planning 211
  selecting objectives 209

exhibitions and trade fairs *cont.*
　selecting venues 210
　visitors book 44
experience/commitment matrix 42, 47
export credits guarantee department – ECGD 125, 177, 181–182
　comprehensive short-term guarantee 182
export intelligence service (EIS) 118
export marketing research scheme – BOTB service 119–121, 146
export representative service – BOTB 122
export/s
　clubs 138
　development costs 52–53, 67
　direction 149
　directories 149–150, 155
　factors 177
　groups and councils 225
　houses 152, 156
　inquiries 43–44, 48–49
　letters 202
　licence 182
　literature 214
　management companies 156–157
　times 149
　training 52
　trips 204
　united 67
ex-works 187

fairs and promotion branch BOTB 121
feed supplement firm 78
finance
　methods of payment 179–181
　post-shipment 179–180
　pre-shipment 176
　smaller exports scheme 180–181
　sources of 177
financial control 20
Financial Times 37–38, 104
fish farming 41–42
food firm 102
foundry firm 75, 135

free on board, FOB 187
freight forwarders, 35, 124–125, 185–186
furniture firms 23, 44, 80, 97, 155, 211, 218

George R & G Burg report on small firms 126–127
gross national product GNP 92
growth 17–28
　growth loop 23
　growth matrix 23, 27
　growth options 19–24

haberdashery firm 156
Henri Lloyd Ltd 210
hints to exporters – BOTB guide 118, 204
holidays 204
Hong Kong Development Council 34

import licensing branch 34
importing, see purchasing
incoterms 136, 187
industrial marketing researchers' check list 120
industrial relations 65–66
industry served/production capability matrix 71
institutes
　of British Architects 153
　of export 138, 168, 179, 187
　of marketing 138
insurance 196
intermediaries *see* agents
intermediate technology industry services 97
international directory of market research organisations 120
international directory of published market research 106, 120, 150
international labour office 102
interpreters 211
invoices 186, 188, 192
　consular invoices 192

jobbing 62
John Mason & Son 94–95

Kompass 171

language 47
  as method of market selection 96
  communication 203
lead times 34
letter of credit 180
libraries 99
  industry research associations 136–137
  local 144–145
  network 145
  product data store – BOTB 119
  science reference library 151
  statistics and market intelligence library 104, 119
  trade associations 133
licensing 21, 36–37, 79, 213
  agreement 36–37
Lloyds 196
Lloyds Bank Economic Survey 99
local authorities 138

mail order 95, 179
managing intermediaries 45
  relationships 117–118
managing promotion 207–216
market attractiveness 107
  attractiveness/company standing matrix 107, 112
market concentration 110, 221
market development 22
market entry 152–174
market entry guarantee scheme – BOTB 122–123
market penetration 20, 27
market prospects service – BOTB 122
market research 141–151
  agency/consultant 147
  basis for decision making 148
  external information 144
  internal information 143a
  matrix 143
  network 145
  objectives 142
  on line databases 144
  primary 146

scanmark 147
society 147
statistics 102, 144, 151
subsidies 146
market segmentation 109–110
market selection 86–112
market spreading 221
marketing 20–21
  definition 29
  myopia 32
mattress firm 77
MBE 60
merchant banks 131
micro-nutrient firm 87
Middle East 15, 78, 167
Midland Bank Trade Brief 99
  small firm exporters scheme 180–181
Ministry of Defence – Defence Sales Organisation 123
Motor Industry Research Association 196
multi-client studies 146

National Economic Development Office – NEDO 125
networks 32, 33–34, 74–85, 129
  banks 130
  ICI 157
  patents 151
non-price factors 207
North of England Development Council – NEDC 185

objectives *see also* planning 53, 54, 115, 142, 167, 206, 208, 209, 220, 223
oil supplies firm 94, 123–124
Oilab Lubrication Ltd 123–124
omnibus surveys 146
order processing 200
Organisation for Economic Cooperation & Development (OECD) 99, 102
outward missions 121
Overseas Status Report Service – BOTB 122

packaging design 24
packaging firm 143, 161–162
packing lists 186, 190
patents 15, 36, 151
payments, methods of 179–181
personnel systems 66
'Piggy-back' exporting 157
planning for exports 217–224
   action plans 221–222
   budgets and controls 222
   getting started 219
   setting objectives 220
   strategy 221
   strengths and weaknesses 223
   using a workshop approach 219
plant assessment 65
plastic ommercial stationery firm 94, 106–107
Plastic Moulding (Cradley) Ltd 65
plastic moulding firm 65
playground equipment firm 24, 56, 107–110
polytechnics – help with information 99, 144
population 90
product
   benefits 62, 64, 214
   concentration 64
   features 64
   range/production capability matrix 70
   rejects 64
   service analysis 62–65
product development 21, 221
production systems 66
Professional Manufacturing & Distribution (PMD) 23–24
profitability 63
Projects and Export Policy Division – BOTB 123
promotion 133–134, 207–216
   budgets 208
   campaigns 215–216
protective coverings firm 54
publicity 123, 212–214
   COI 123, 213
   directories 151
   EIBIS 213–214

press releases 212
pump firm 97
purchasing 29–40
   agreement 35
   definition 29–30
   how to 33–34
   reasons for 32

quality circles 66
quality standards 64
Queen's Award to Industry for Exports 50, 60

research associations, industry 136–137
   Packaging Industry Research Association (PIRA) 137
resources, mobilising of 61–73
   audit 66, 73
retail promotions 121
risk reduction 119
Road Haulage Association 196
Rockhurst Design Services 55
royalty payments 36
rubber/moulding firm 22, 95, 153, 167, 203

sales force 55
sales volume/market growth matrix 108
Scottish Council (Development & Industry) 126
Scottish Development Agency 125
seminars and symposia – BOTB support for 121
Siemens 213
Simplification of International Trade Procedure (SITPRO) 124, 196–197, 198
small firms – advantages of size 51
sport equipment firms 31, 145, 168, 202
Standard Industrial Classification – SIC 145
standards see British Standards Institute
steel stockholder 54, 152
Stores of the World, see directories 155

strategic choice 24–25
strategy 221, 224
strength and weakness – analysis 68, 73, 223
subcontracting 153
subsidies 120, 121, 137, 211
suppliers 29–40, 79
support agencies 113–140
synchronize production 54, 55, 60

tariffs 118, 133
team work 66, 67
Technical Help for Exports (THE) 106, 137
technology gap 97, 108
   technology gap/ease of access matrix 97
telephone interviewing 146
telex *see* communications
test certificates 196
   facilities 137
textile firms 154, 163–164
time zones 96–97
Times Atlas of the World 97
TIR carnets 196

trade associations 132–134
trade fairs *see* exhibitions
trade missions 134
training 52, 64, 174, 200
travel agents 97, 186, 204
trip reports 173–174
   objectives
turn-around time 206

United Nations economic surveys 99, 102
universities – help with information 99, 144
user segmentation 109, 110

vertical outward trade missions 134

Wicksteed 32, 56, 68, 107–110
Wireless World 213
working capital 67
World Aid Section – BOTB service 118
World Bank 118

Yellow pages 171